Why Good People Can't Leave Bad Relationships

LETTING GO OF YOUR SIX SO-CALLED GOOD TRAITS
THAT KEEP YOU TIED TO THE DEVIL YOU KNOW

CINDI SANSONE-BRAFF

Disclaimer

The intent of the author is only to offer accurate and authoritative information in regard to the subject matter covered. This book is sold with the understanding that the author is not rendering legal, accounting, psychiatric, or other professional service. The information contained in this book is in no way intended to serve as a replacement for professional therapy. Any use of the information contained in this publication is done so at the reader's discretion, and the author and the publisher disclaim any and all liability and responsibility for the reader's actions.

CreateSpace Independent Publishing Platform
North Charleston, South Carolina

Dedication

For my beloved husband, TJ Clemente
Your love keeps taking me higher…

Author's Note

In order to protect the privacy of my clients whose stories are included in this book, I have changed their names and other identifying characteristics. A small number of individuals described are composites.

Contents

Top Ten Reasons Why You Need This Book Now!

Please answer true or false:

1. I like to see the good in everyone, and I give everyone the benefit of the doubt.
2. I believe everyone is like me and tells the truth, or at least when they're lying, they know that they're lying.
3. I believe I can fix people, and I feel bad when I can't, because somehow I feel it's all my fault anyway.
4. I forgive easily and often.
5. I am extremely loyal.
6. I feel bad when I have to walk away from people, even when they've hurt me.
7. I'm a peacemaker and rarely express anger, even when people have hurt and betrayed me.
8. I tend to turn the other cheek; therefore, I make a lot of excuses for people's abuse: you know, I feel bad that they had bad parents, blah, blah, blah, yada yada yada...
9. I never make people account for their bad actions, so, everyone gets away with murder around me.
10. I'm a giver, and I really don't expect much in return.

After reading the above statements, and answering true to all or most of them, you're now thinking: *Wow! I really am a nice person!* Think again. These personality traits are the ones that keep you trapped in unhappy and unhealthy relationships. Reading this book will give you the strength and courage to know when enough is enough!

You will be shocked to learn that the above traits are a form of *narcissism*. What, me a narcissist? Yes, good people have their own form of narcissism, but I will refer to you as a **"*Well-Meaning Narcissist*,"** as opposed to a **"*Self-Serving Narcissist*."**

Having the above personality traits may make you look like a saint, a Christian martyr, but isn't it egotistical of you to think that you can fix people and that all the mess of the world is your fault?

If you possess any one of the traits listed in the above ten statements, or, what's worse—many of these traits—then you really, really need this book!

Beg, borrow, Kindle it!

Still Not Sure If You Need This Book?
A Quick Quiz

Answer as honestly as you can with either a yes or a no.
(You can also answer with a long song and dance, if you'd like.)

1. Have you ever kept someone in your life even after you caught this person stealing from you?

2. Have you ever kept someone in your life even after you caught that person cheating on you sexually with a number of other people?

3. Have you ever kept someone working for you when he or she wasn't doing his or her job because you felt sorry for this person?

4. Have you kept someone in your life (spouse, sibling, child, employee, etc.) even after you caught this person forging your name?

5. Have you kept family members or friends in your life who are drug addicts, alcoholics, spendaholics, or gamblers, even when these people have continually reneged on their promises to get help, and even though their addictions continued to hurt you emotionally, physically, psychologically, or financially?

6. Have you loaned a family member or friend money even though this person still owes you money that he or she has never bothered to pay back?

7. In business, have you continued to do work for someone even though this person still owes you money from previous work that you have completed?

8. Have you ever fallen for someone who came on like a Prince or Princess in the beginning of the relationship, and then later found out that this person truly turned out to be a Beast?

9. Have you ever fallen in love with someone and later found out that this person lied about everything, including his or her financial or marital situation?

10. Do you always seem to get involved in relationships with people who need fixing?

11. Has anyone ever lied right to your face, and even though your gut told you something wasn't kosher, you still chose to believe this person?

12. Have you ever been involved personally or professionally with someone who turned out to be a pathological liar?

13. Do you find yourself making excuses for other people's abuse?

14. Have you ever been with someone you thought was honest and good, and later found out that he or she was a sociopath or—worse yet—a psychopath?

15. Have you ever gotten involved in a long-distance Internet love affair with someone, only to find out that this person was nothing like he or she pretended to be?

16. Have you ever been on an online dating site only to discover that seven out of ten people you met were sex addicts, commitment-phobes, or just plain crazy?

17. Did you ever get involved with someone who seemed honest at first, but then later ripped you off in some way—say, for instance, ringing up your credit card without your approval?

18. Are you always bailing someone out of some kind of mess?

19. Do you seem to have more than your share of people who come into your life with sob stories, and you end up feeling as if it's your job to fix their situations?

20. Have you ever gotten involved with the kind of people who take all and give nothing?

21. Do you find yourself forgiving others time and time again, even when they keep committing the same sins against you?

22. Are you too hard on yourself?

If you've answered more than two questions with a yes, then don't even think about putting this book down!

The Good Powers of the universe are infinitely more powerful than the evil ones. Sadly, on earth, for far too long, the bad guys have greatly outnumbered the good guys. Armed with an arsenal of tools—righteous thoughts, righteous words, and righteous actions—the crucified minority, once and for all, shall inherit the earth.

—Cindi Sansone-Braff

Introduction

Have you ever wondered how a nice, honest, and reasonably sane person like yourself ended up with the life from hell? Have you ever kicked yourself in the head because you didn't see the writing on the wall with an employee, employer, lover, friend, family member, or—worse yet—your own spouse, and then, as a direct result of this person's bad choices, you found yourself emotionally, physically, psychologically, spiritually, and/or financially bankrupt?

Do you feel like the inspiration for the Barnum and Bailey saying "a sucker is born every minute"? Do people treat you like a doormat? Are you a giver, and yet, everyone else in your life operates under the "take all and give nothing principle"? Are you starting to feel like a martyr? Are you always rescuing someone? And why is it that when you finally get fed up with these moochers and stop giving, they forget all that you have ever done for them? Have you ever wondered why these "what have you done for me lately people" always seem to be magnetically drawn to you?

Why is it that everyone you've ever loved seems to hurt or betray you? What is it that the universe keeps trying to show you that you just don't seem to get? Why is it that you assume everyone thinks like you do? Why is it that you believe that others will do unto you as they would want done unto themselves? Everyone knows that you're the kind of a person whose word is gospel and whose handshake is as good as a signed contract. And yet those so-called wonderful traits of yours have come back to bite you in the butt more times than you'd like to remember. Why are you so trusting of others that you take what they say at face value, and you never bother to check up on them or fact check what they've told you? Why is it that you always feel that you must give everyone the benefit of the doubt?

This book is meant to rip off your blinders and get you to see what you haven't wanted to see. In reading this book, you'll learn that at this stage of human evolution, only 30 percent of the people you meet are genuinely good human beings. *Wait a minute...Did I read the last sentence correctly?* Yes, the sad truth is that you read it correctly the first time, and you didn't need to bother reading it a second time. What this means is—if only 30 percent of the people you encounter are genuinely trying to be good, then 70 percent of the people you encounter are manipulators of one kind or another. Yes, of course, some are sweeter and dumber manipulators than others; therefore, more benign than other kinds of manipulators, but manipulation is manipulation no matter how you slice it.

On another note, we can all get on our knees and give thanks that most people aren't smart enough and evil enough to be like Hitler, but yes, this level of manipulation still exists on this planet. No wonder we often feel taken advantage of and deceived. Yet, how is it that we never seem to learn to watch our own backs?

Oh, I hear you asking, how did she come up with this figure that boils down to seven out of ten people just aren't all that great? I came to this conclusion through observing my life and the people who have been in it, and by observing the lives of the more than ten thousand people I have guided throughout the last two decades. You can come up with your own accounting on this one—but first, you have to get the blinders off and see people for who they truly are—before you start counting. I would love for you to prove me wrong. That would mean the world is changing for the better!

Now, the next couple of questions that I'm going to throw your way are going to make you cringe. You'll clearly see that people who are good to a fault are actually good to the point of insanity. For instance, do you have trouble speaking up for yourself because you want everyone to like you—even people you can't stand, and people you have absolutely no respect for? (Come on, you've got to laugh out loud over the ridiculousness of that one!) Why is it that nice people want everyone to like them? If you think about it, why would you care if your deadbeat brother, who robbed you blind of your inheritance, likes you?

Have you continued to be loyal to people who have stabbed you in the back time and time again? (If that doesn't sound certifiable, I don't know what is!) Do you make peace at any price? In other words, do you shut the hell up in order to avoid confrontation? Have you turned the other cheek so many times that you continually feel like you're being slapped silly?

Have you ever wondered why so many of the lessons you learned in Sunday School, such as "See the good in others," "Give everyone the benefit of the doubt," "Help others selflessly," and "Be humble and don't toot your own horn," have yielded such poor results? Has it ever occurred to you that these "angelic" traits of yours are the root of so many of your troubles?

You're a reasonable person and smart enough, right? Then how is it that you've made some really dumb choices as far as picking friends, lovers, or business partners? Why is that you keep getting involved with some of the biggest losers, liars, and louses in the universe? Have you had more than your share of romantic partners who have cheated on you? What is it that you're not seeing? Why can't you just see what's really in front of your face?

If you really don't want to know the answers to the above questions, and if you really don't want to stop playing the victim, then put this book down right now, and go watch

TV. Most of the shows produced on television right now will reinforce all the nonsense that keeps you trapped to an unhappy life. *The Self-Serving Narcissists* seem to come out on top on television. But, if you really want to have a life that you love, one in which you're the master of your destiny, then read on. In no time, this book will open your eyes, get you to toss your rose-colored glasses out the window, and have you seeing the red flags that you've been missing all along. Just remember: *there are no victims, only volunteers.*

Do you feel as if you're always carrying everyone else's crosses? Then you'll love the chapter called "Your Belief That You Are Your Brother's Keeper." I call *The Good-to-a-Fault People,* who carry everyone else's crosses and clean up everybody else's messes, *The Great Enablers.* This chapter should throw a huge bucket of cold water on your belief that it's your job to fix everything and everyone. You'll learn why you can't change anyone or fix people unless they want to fix themselves. Sure, you can be a messenger. You can play show-and-tell with others and help them see the error of their ways. If they don't get it, then you have a right to deliver another message to them by walking away and leaving them where they fall. Hey, with any luck at all, by the time you leave this earth, you may even learn to change yourself and fix what's wrong with you.

News flash: if you think that letting that deadbeat brother of yours get away with robbing you blind is a virtue, this book is going to be like electroshock to your soul. In accordance with the fixed laws of Karma, you will be held accountable in your afterlife for allowing your brother to go on thinking that stealing from others, particularly stealing from people who love and trust you, goes unpunished. Every person your deadbeat brother robs from that day forward will go on your soul records as crimes that you may have had the power to stop. Had you allowed your brother to suffer the full consequences of his actions, he may not have committed any further crimes of that nature again.

You'll get no brownie points from God for carrying your brother's cross or for being a martyr.

This book will teach you the real *Beauty and the Beast* story, because we all know that Disney lied. You'll see why it's rarely the Beast—the diehard alcoholic or hard-core drug addict—who becomes the Prince or Princess. Yes, it happens. Miracles can and do happen, but they're the rare exceptions and not the rule. And these kinds of miracles are earned by that person through his or her own good graces and inner and outer changes. You can't wish nor will someone to make a miraculous change, no matter how hard you pray or how hard you try. Stop thinking that you're a miracle worker, because you're not. In the reality version of the *Beauty and the Beast* fairy tale, things happen the other way around—it's the Prince or Princess who becomes the Beast, and we all know from firsthand experience that these beastly people break our hearts and often our bank accounts at the same time. Rest assured; by the time you finish reading this book, you will have mastered the art of quickly recognizing the wolf in sheep's clothing so that you will never be fooled again—not for long, anyway!

Do you find yourself chronically depressed because your life situation never seems to change no matter what you do? Has it ever occurred to you that you're a nice person who is depressed because you keep turning anger inward instead of placing it where it belongs? This book will help you to get in touch with your buried anger and get you to understand that anger—righteous anger or divine anger, that is—is not only a valid emotion to feel when someone has hurt or betrayed you, but it's the only *sane* thing to feel under those circumstances.

Have you ever asked yourself, "Why am I plagued with guilt and anxiety, even though I've never intentionally done a bad thing in my entire life?" Do you do countless numbers of things you don't want to do just because you feel guilty if you don't? Do the people around you know how to push your guilt buttons to get what they want? Have you been noticing lately that the good people around you seem to be plagued with an enormous amount of free-floating guilt, whereas the mean SOB.s never seem to feel the slightest tinge of guilt or remorse? In that case, you definitely need to keep reading this book to find out when you should feel guilty and when you might just have to walk away from someone or a situation in spite of unearned guilt.

By now, we've all heard that there's a strong mind/body connection. Why is it that some very selfish, greedy people never seem to get sick or suffer? Why doesn't God punish them? How did Hitler's bodyguard, Rochus Misch, who was in the bunker when Hitler killed himself, live to the ripe old age of ninety-six? Till his dying breath on September 5, 2013, SS Staff Sergeant Misch was proud of it all and still claimed that Hitler was "a wonderful boss." Why do the good die young or get sick? Why is it that evil people seem to have nine lives? Do you realize that all the betrayals, anger turned inward, and crosses you carry that are not your own can cause major autoimmune disorders, heart disease, and even cancer? What the mind denies, the body brings forth as illness.

The following information is from an article entitled "Chronic Anger May Lead to Early Death," published December 20, 1990, by Natalie Angier, *New York Times* News Service. This article cited an eighteen-year study about the long-term health effects of chronic anger on women conducted by Dr. Mara Julius, an epidemiologist at the University of Michigan. Dr. Julius discovered that "For many women, constant suppressed anger seems to be a stronger risk factor of early mortality than smoking."

Do you forgive too quickly and too often, even when people keep doing the same damn things to you over and over again? In The New Testament when Peter asked Jesus, "Lord, how often shall my brother sin against, and I forgive him? Until seven times?" Jesus answered, "I don't tell you until seven times, but until seventy times seven" (Matthew 18:21–22). OK, that's a lot of times, but he didn't say a gazillion times. Nor do we have to forgive the same sin done unto us, time and time again. This book will teach you how, when, and under what circumstances and conditions true forgiveness may be granted. You'll also learn that you can forgive the people who have trespassed against you, but that doesn't mean that you have to forgive their actions. Keep reading and you'll learn why saying "I'm sorry" isn't a license for people to go on doing whatever they want without suffering any real consequences for their continually hurtful behaviors. You'll learn how people manipulate you into forgiving them just because they've told you the truth or even just one-tenth of the truth, and why your very sanity depends upon your ability to walk away from these kinds of manipulators before they drag you down the road to ruin.

Perhaps the most important thing you'll learn from reading this book is the following: if you don't learn to leave people where they fall, to stop making excuses for their abuse, and to stop being loyal to people who don't deserve your loyalty, you will keep being given life experiences and people who will hurt, betray, and ultimately destroy you, until you finally learn enough is enough! By the time you finish reading this book, I hope you'll stop being one of **The Great Enablers** and be well onto your way to being one of **The Enlightened Ones.**

Have you ever wondered why bad things happen to good people? In a nutshell, if you keep carrying everybody's crosses, and keep cleaning up *their* messes, God has no choice but to wreck havoc on *your* world so that you'll get out of God's way. Sure, everyone is entitled to one rehab, one get-out-of-jail-free card, one time his or her life is a sinking Titanic. After that, your job is to leave that person where he or she falls. Let go and let God take care of that mess.

This book will teach you that you are responsible *only* for *your* behavior. That it's not your responsibility to "fix everything and everyone." You will in fact learn that it's a very narcissistic way of being to think that everything is *your* fault or *your* responsibility. (What, me narcissistic? Why, I only think of others!) You may be surprised by what this book will reveal about your own need to be needed, and how that neediness is keeping you tied to needy people.

You'll also find out why "hiding your head in the sand" is one of the worst possible things you can do. Yes, sometimes problems are like snowstorms. And even if you live in upstate New York, eventually the snow will melt, so you could, theoretically, do nothing to clear it away. But other problems are more like toothaches. If you neglect them, they only get worse. This little survival guide will teach you how to face what you must face and do what you must do, so that you can get on with the pursuit of happiness.

Oh, yeah, and if you're a Dyson for dirtbags, then you certainly need to read this book. Memorizing it would be even better.

This book will also reveal why your need to make peace at any price has made your life a battleground. In addition, you'll come to realize why **The Great Enablers**, with their inability to punish or seek retribution for what has been done to them, are one reason why so much injustice exists in the world. **The Self-Serving Narcissists,** whom I have dubbed **The Unfixables,** have learned this lesson from **The Great Enablers** of the world: Crime pays, especially if you rob, rape, and pillage those closest to you.

Perhaps the greatest gift that will come out of reading this book is this: you will learn how to avoid stepping into the traps that **The Unfixables** are masters of setting. You will no longer be blinded by their keen ability to listen well to what you have to say when they first meet you in order to scope you out. Once they've absorbed what you have to say and what you profess to want, then they begin systematically echoing it all back to you, giving you the false impression that they think just like you do and that they want what you want. Later on, they'll never listen to a single word you ever have to say. You'll also notice that these same people, at first, come on like the "rescuers." They'll do something you need, and then, you—if you are *The Good-to-a-Fault Person*—feel indebted to them for the rest of your life. After the initial rescue, they'll never do a damn thing to help you ever again, but still you remain loyal to them, no matter how much they hurt or betray you later on. This book will teach you just how dysfunctional this kind of thinking really is.

Most definitely, this book is "the good person's survival guide" in a bad, bad, bad, bad world. A great deal of the information you read here will seem counterrevolutionary, because it contradicts a lot of the teachings you learned in Sunday school. All advances in human consciousness always sound and feel revolutionary at first. There was a time in history when beating your child—the "spare the rod and spoil the child" mind-set—was the accepted mode of disciplining children. Those parents who still beat their children today are doing what historically was the norm, and they haven't yet come up to speed with the higher consciousness thought that corporal punishment is unacceptable, and in many instances, even criminal in nature. So, let the new revolution, toward a new quantum leap in human evolution, begin with you.

Finally, you will learn that your mantra is this: It's not OK that you did this to me.

The case studies in this book are based on people I have had the privilege of guiding and assisting in their quests for better relationships. The names and certain identifying particulars have been changed to protect confidentiality and to protect the privacy of these individuals.

The most important case study of all in this book is your own, so please answer the question sections to the best of your ability. The best way to read this book is by engaging as many of your senses as possible. If you own a copy of this book, feel free to highlight and mark up any and all sections that pertain to you. Add your own thoughts and epiphanies in the margins. Keep this book close to you at all times, so that you can refer to it often, especially if and when you find yourself falling back into your old patterns of behavior.

Warning: once again, let me state that if you're not ready for real change, or if you want to keep playing the victim card, then put this book down right away and run back to your old life. But please, then stop bitching about your life and know that in the end we get the lives we choose. If you keep making the same bad choices and getting the same bad results, don't blame the gods or other people, blame only yourself, from this day forward. And remember what Albert Einstein once said—"Insanity: doing the same thing over and over again and expecting different results."

Be prepared to learn some *New Golden Rules* that will help us, collectively, build a brave new world.

My intention in writing this book is not to offend, but rather to awaken.

A special thanks to *The World English Bible (WEB),* a public-domain modern English translation of the *Holy Bible,* for the biblical quotations used in this book.

Your prayer from this day forward: "Dear Lord, I pray that you may teach me how to do what's best for everyone, including myself."

Amen!

One

Things You Need to Know before We Start

Holding on to a person, place, or thing for too long and not taking action to move forward soon enough is the root of half of the troubles in this world. Acting impulsively, without thinking strategically, is the root of the other half of the troubles we experience. Learning when to hold and when to fold is the key to mastering life.

—Cindi Sansone-Braff

Everyone manipulates. All humans act and sound like used car salesmen at one time or another, as they try to get others to: buy what they're selling, see the world the way they want them to see it, or get them to do what they want. Manipulation is something each and every one of us does each and every day of our lives. Some of us do it with the belief that we truly know what's best for others. Others do it to get what they want, with little thought of whom or what they may be throwing under the bus.

The truth of the matter is this: we all have to be aware of our own tendencies to manipulate others.

There are degrees of manipulation like anything else. But as you read this chapter, I urge you to see if you're guilty of any of the different kinds of manipulations and games people play, and vow to work at being more honest, yet strategic, in your dealings with others. Strategy implies that you have a plan. Try to affect people and deliver your messages to others in a strategic manner that is backed by truth, facts, and love. Temper your honesty with kindness and be willing to put your money where your mouth is. Strive to use no blind threats, no coercion, no hissy fits or temper tantrums to get your way. Remember that facts speak volumes.

In being strategic, you are using well-thought-out and well-planned maneuvers in your dealing with individuals and situations. When you're dealing with manipulative people, you have no choice but to formulate a plan of action. This plan would include a vision of the outcome you desire, an awareness of the manipulative techniques others are utilizing, a careful analysis of the situation, and time for gathering any information you may need to see your vision through. If you act impulsively and rashly with manipulators, you will only hang yourself. Be patient, thorough, calm, and steadfast in dealing with these kinds of people, and you will come out virtuous and victorious in the long run.

By the time you finish reading this book, it's my greatest hope that you'll learn how to use your knowledge, actions, and words to create more loving and satisfying relationships in your life, both personally and professionally, while avoiding the art of manipulation.

Knowing When Someone Is Fixable and When Someone Isn't

If someone is manipulative, there's still hope that you may be able to affect this person and get him or her to see things your way. If someone is highly judgmental there is hope here, too, that this person might change.

News flash: if a person is manipulative, judgmental, and sees the world through a self-serving, narcissistic lens, run for the hills. These people cannot see beyond their own shadows. These kinds of people might appear to change when they're in the midst of a major wake-up call such as illness, jail time, financial ruin—in other words, when the gun is at their heads. As soon as the wake-up call subsides, these people go back to their manipulative/judgmental/narcissistic ways. There is, of course, hope for all people, but these people would need to earn a miracle, and for the most part, their thoughts, actions, and behaviors aren't going to earn a miracle. Stop trying to be a *Miracle Worker*, and learn to strategically walk away from the self-serving, manipulative, judgmental narcissists of the world.

Keep in mind that there's always a greater chance of someone changing for the better if the person is under the age of twenty-five. People's brain chemistry and behaviors start getting set in stone by the time they've been on the planet for a quarter of a century, and the odds of them miraculously changing get slimmer and slimmer with each passing year.

A Vicious Game People Play: The Deadly Triangle

Before we get into the four kinds of people who exist on the earth, we need to discuss a deadly game that *all people play*: the victim/rescuer/persecutor triangle. This game or behavior pattern is so prevalent that after I point it out to you, you're going to have an "aha moment" where you're going to say, "*How did I miss that one for all these years?*"

Transactional Analysis is a highly effective program created by a California psychiatrist named Eric Berne that teaches people that we are responsible for what happens to us in the future, regardless of what has happened to us in the past. This groundbreaking therapy was later translated into easy-to-understand terms by Berne's disciple, Thomas Harris, in the bestselling book *I'm OK—You're OK,* which I highly recommend that every person on this planet read in our first step toward a saner universe. This book was a life-changing read for me. It made people's dysfunctional patterns of behavior so much clearer to me, as I saw the victim/rescuer/persecutor triangle play itself out—everywhere I looked. Unfortunately, this is a vicious psychological game that we've all learned to master. Expertly, each and every one of us moves around this deadly triangle playing three recurring roles: that of the victim, the rescuer, or the persecutor, each and every day, if not each and every waking hour, of our lives.

The following excerpt from my book *Grant Me a Higher Love: How to Go from the Relationship from Hell to One That's Heaven Sent by Scaling The Ladder of Love* (pages 124–26), gives an example of the victim/rescuer/persecutor triangle.

A husband comes home from work and screams at his wife, "The house is a pigsty; the kids are running around like wild maniacs, and why the hell isn't dinner on the table?" (He is the persecutor.) The obviously exhausted wife starts crying. (She is the victim.) Then the husband suddenly acts caring and hugs her. (He becomes the rescuer.)

A moment later the wife starts screaming back at her husband, "You don't give a damn about me. All you care about is yourself. Did you ever stop to think what my day was like?" (Now the wife has taken on the role of the persecutor.) Then her husband gets irate, complaining about how hard he worked all day and how nothing he ever does is good enough for her. (He is now taking on the role of the victim.)

He runs out the door, heading to the nearest bar, while his wife starts crying and screaming, "How could you run out and leave me like this?" (Now she's the victim again.) His wife then starts chasing after him, saying she's sorry. (She has taken on the role of rescuer.)

From this all-too-familiar scenario we can see how the husband went from screaming at his wife—in other words, persecuting her—to hugging her or rescuing her, to feeling so victimized (persecuted) and abused by her that fleeing seems the only alternative. The wife went from feeling abused or victimized, to feeling rescued, to becoming the angry persecutor, to becoming re-victimized again as the husband angrily runs out the door, and as she chases after him, she plays the role of the rescuer trying to save the day. Does any of this ring true to you?

Do any or many of your interactions with people follow this pattern? If so, you have to consciously choose to step out of this deadly triangle and begin to respond calmly. Learn to answer the question *straight* even if it was a loaded one meant to set you off. A sense of humor goes a long way to diffuse the situation when someone has thrown you an angry hook.

For the next few weeks, pay close attention to the way you habitually respond to people. Nice people seem to think there's nothing wrong with regularly playing the role of the rescuer/martyr. Just remember that the rescuer might be the nicer part of this deadly triangle, but it's dysfunctional all the same.

Which role in the deadly triangle are you most often cast in—the victim, the persecutor, or the rescuer?

Understanding the Role that Archetypes Play in the Roles We Play in Life

Archetypes are primordial images that have been deeply ingrained in our collective unconscious. These primordial images are like shorthand symbols our subconscious minds use to communicate with us. For instance, the very sight of some archetypal images, including the ocean, the stars, the sun, the desert, or a mountain, convey a mood, a meaning, or an emotion to all human beings. Archetypes can also be recurring personality types, stereotypical in nature, that are common to a culture, people, and, to a large extent, all human beings. These recurring characters are stored in our collective unconscious and serve to reveal the different paths and life choices we can make. Some archetypes are positive ones, such as that of the "Hero" and the "Healer," while still others can be negative ones, such as the "Con Artist" and the "Gossip."

These recurring archetypal characters appear in mythology, in our dreams, in fairy tales, movies, literature, and artwork, and are easy types for humans to identify with. Some common archetypes are: the "Princess," the "Clown," the "Wise Old Man," the "Hobo," and the "Damsel in Distress," to name but a few.

All of us live out many archetypes during our lifetimes, and they serve as the building blocks for our lives. For example, a woman might be a medical doctor by profession, thereby living out the archetype of the "Healer," but she might also be a mother; therefore, she is also living out the archetype of the "Matriarch." On top of this, she might be a writer, and in that case she's living out the archetype of the "Artist" as well.

Who's the Boss?

Most human beings, at this stage of human evolution, still play out the negative archetype of "Master/Slave."

6

The Master/Slave archetype is often played out symbolically between men and women. Even in this day and age of women's liberation, many women still take on the subservient role in the household, regardless of how powerful they might be in the outside world. The antiquated notion that the man is king of the castle was continually reinforced throughout human history with its patriarchal societies. Modern-day men and women both have to vigilantly monitor their behavior to keep this archetype from doing its insidious damage to their relationships. For example, a recent study indicated that in many marriages the man is still the master of the finances, even though women often make as much money as their husbands do, or even more—and then women try to even the score by controlling when the couple have sex.

The Master/Slave archetype is also often reenacted in the boss/employee relationship and the parent/child relationship.

Modern couples have to work hard to treat each other as two equals. As a relationship coach, I have observed that the single biggest sin that seems to tear couples apart is the playing out of the Master/Slave archetype.

This archetype can be enacted between couples in several ways. Firstly, there are those partners who truly believe that they own their mates; therefore, they have the right to control their mates' every thought and deed. There is a lot of raping of boundaries in these relationships in which the partners who have crowned themselves emperor or empress feel that they have the right to tell their mates how to spend money, who to see, what to wear, and basically when to jump up and when to step down. In due time, the slave will rebel. At this point, either the tables will turn with the slave mate now becoming the master, or the relationship comes to an end when the enslaved mate finds the courage or support to flee.

The flip side of this archetype is when one partner takes on the role of Mommy or Daddy to the other partner, who has a Peter Pan complex. This is a buzz kill to sex and romance, because the partner who takes on the role of parenting the perennial child will eventually grow tired of babysitting and coddling an overgrown baby who either can't or won't grow up. In turn, the babied partner begins to rebel against and resent the parenting partner, and the power struggles, temper tantrums, and reprimands eventually lead to the demise of the relationship.

True Soul Mate relationships take place between two people who are equals in their partnership, and who could, if necessary, stand on their own two feet, emotionally, psychologically, spiritually, and financially.

Understanding and recognizing this Master/Slave archetype and the role you regularly take on, is one giant step forward to having healthy relationships, both personally and professionally.

A New Kind of Twenty-First Century Master/Slave Archetype: The Commitment-Phobes Calling All the Shots

Commitment-phobia has reached epidemic proportions and appears to be a highly contagious phenomenon. I really can't do justice to this enormous topic in this book, and if you wish to know more about this issue, please read Step 17 in my book *Grant Me a Higher Love: How to Go from the Relationship from Hell to One That's Heaven Sent by Scaling The Ladder of Love.*

Having observed thousands of people stuck in relationships that seem to be going nowhere fast, I can tell you that the one trait that all true commitment-phobes possess is a high level of narcissism. They don't care how their inability to commit is hurting others. They don't care that they're breaking other people's hearts or causing them undue stress and angst. Commitment-phobes are busy protecting themselves from real or imagined hurts, and that's as far as their self-serving lenses can see.

How this fear of commitment plays itself out in terms of the Master/Slave archetype is simple: the person who fears commitment holds all the power. Commitment-phobes basically tell their mates when to come close and when to go, and they let their mates know "whatever you do—don't call me; I'll call you." This is the worst kind of enactment of Master/Slave, since it forces people to take an awful lot of crap in the name of love. Commitment-phobes leave their mates feeling powerless.

The main warning sign that you're dealing with a commitment-phobic person is your gut feeling that every time you appear to get closer to this person, he or she suddenly becomes unavailable or begins acting evasively and emotionally distant for no apparent reason. Commitment-phobes leave their partners feeling like they never know if or when they'll ever see each other again.

Dealing with commitment-phobes makes you crazy because of the level of mixed messages given, and because you're left feeling that you have no control over the situation. When you're dealing with diehard commitment-phobes, they call all the shots, and you're at their mercy and beck and call. Basically you become enslaved to the whims and dictates of a commitment-phobe. This kind of "now I want you, now I don't" yo-yoing behavior can go on forever, leaving people feeling as helpless and abused as any slave has ever felt.

If you're currently in this situation, it's up to you to call your partner on his or her behavior. You give this person a choice: either commit to me with your entire heart, soul, mind, and body and commit to healing, or find another sucker to do your long-term destructive dance with.

Basically, it boils down to you telling this person—it's all or nothing. If the commitment-phobe chooses to walk away, that still doesn't mean it's over. You have to stand firm on your decision and resist talking, texting, booty-calling, or interacting with this person on any level, except in a full-fledged, committed way.

If you stand by your guns, this commitment-phobe may see that he or she fears losing you more than loving you, and later may come back ready, willing, and able to commit. You just have to be sure if the commitment-phobe does resurface that you once again state how you feel by saying, "What's your intention in contacting me? Is it to stick two feet into this relationship and make it work? If not, I can't do this."

Ellen, the Master, and Daniel, the Slave

Daniel had just turned thirty when I met him for the very first time. He came to see me for a relationship reading that was actually gifted to him by his sister. He wasn't sure what to expect, or even sure if he wanted to be here, but he said, "At this point, I'm so tired of jumping through hoops to make my wife happy, I'm willing to try anything to ease the pain."

Daniel, in tears, told me that after five years of marriage, Ellen was ready to call it quits. Daniel might have been more receptive to just letting her move on, but he was concerned about how their divorce would affect their four-year-old daughter.

Daniel had known Ellen most of his adult life. They had met while they were still in high school, and they had been with each other on and off ever since. When they first met at a school dance, Daniel's mother had just divorced his overbearing, control freak, womanizing father, and Daniel shared a lot of the angst he was going through with Ellen.

He told her how he hated his father with every fiber of his being for all the years of battering and beatings he had inflicted upon his mother. Back in the day, Ellen was a good listener. She seemed to understand what Daniel was going through, since she had witnessed her own parents' brutal divorce, which hit like a tornado after her mother got caught cheating on her father with her personal trainer.

Daniel had sworn to himself that he would never turn into his father. He always tried to treat Ellen with reverence and respect. He never bossed her around or told her what to do. His friends used to laugh at him and say, "Ellen's got you by the balls. She says 'Jump,' and you say 'How high.'"

It was never Daniel who instigated the off times in their relationship. It was always Ellen, but the breakups never lasted more than a few months. Ellen would always return without much explanation as to why she had left in the first place, or why she had returned later on. Daniel's friends told him that he was an idiot, and that Ellen always broke up with him when she found someone new, and when that fling fizzled out, she returned with her tail between her legs. Ellen always insisted there was never anyone else; she just needed some time to find herself.

When Ellen broke things off shortly before their wedding, Daniel told her, "You pull this crap again and it's over for good this time." Ellen replied, "You do what you've got to do. But I've got to be 100 percent sure that if and when I walk down the aisle with you, it's the right thing to do. You know that I never want to get a divorce, and I know you never want to get one either."

During that monthlong breakup, Daniel was sick to his stomach worrying about whether he should cancel the wedding or not, but in his heart of hearts, he hoped she would return, even though he'd made it clear to her that he'd never take her back again.

One night his best friend, Adam, showed up at Daniel's apartment with a picture he had snapped the night before in the local bar where they all used to hang out. Daniel was shocked to see Ellen kissing another guy, and yet, he still couldn't pull the plug on the wedding and moped around like a motherless child.

A week later, Ellen returned saying, "I'm ready to marry you." When Daniel showed her the picture of her kissing the other guy, she said, "That was just a joke. My sister dared me to go up to that guy and plant a wet one on him. It didn't mean anything." Looking back, Daniel wondered how he could have believed Ellen in the first place. Adam refused to attend the wedding, and Daniel found himself scrambling around to find someone else to be his best man. Ellen's brother stepped up to the plate to do it, and the wedding went off without a hitch.

I asked Daniel, "What's your gut telling you about Ellen and her latest need to walk away from you?"

Daniel said, "I don't know. I don't know what to think. She says there's no one else. It's about us, and how we don't see eye to eye on anything, and how she feels that I give all my time and attention to our daughter, and there's nothing left for her."

"Is that true?" I asked.

"I don't know. She always says she's working all this overtime, and I feel bad that our daughter doesn't get to see her mother, so maybe I'm just overcompensating."

"Do you think that your wife has a new man in the picture?"

"She says no, but everyone else is telling me to get the blinders off. Several of our friends and family members have told me that they keep seeing her out and about with her boss, Larry. She says they're just friends, and most of the time when she's with him, it's work related."

"Do you have any reason to suspect that there's more going on?" I asked.

"Yes, I saw a text message from Larry that described a sexual encounter they had, but when I asked her about it, she told me I had no right to spy on her. She accused me of being just like my father, controlling and condescending. She basically told me that if I ever check up on her and treat her like my property again, she'll divorce me, and I'll never see our daughter again."

"Daniel, your wife's a *Self-Serving Narcissist* or what I call one of *The Unfixables.* She twists and turns the truth and never takes responsibility for her own actions. She's also highly judgmental and she's over the age of twenty-five. At this point, she's not likely to change. The chance of you fixing this relationship is pretty slim, since you may not be able to fix her. For instance, she accuses you of being like your father, when she has no idea that she has become her mother, the cheater."

He said, "I just need to let this ride itself out."

"Daniel, what would you tell your daughter to do, if she were in the same situation?"

"I would tell her to try and fix the marriage or leave it."

"Daniel, then that's what I'm advising you to do. Go home, and give her a choice. She can choose your marriage, or she can choose to leave it, but she has to make up her mind."

Ellen told Daniel that night that there was nothing going on with her boss, and that she and Larry only texted each other or talked if they had something work related to discuss. She insisted that she was committed to their marriage and that she was sorry for giving him the impression that she was thinking of leaving. Daniel's gut told him that she was lying. Ellen continued to spend a great deal of after-work time with her boss, and the texting at times went on nonstop, even in the middle of the night.

Six months later, when I saw Daniel for another reading, he was at his wit's end. He didn't know how much more of Ellen's behaviors he could take. Every time he tried to talk to her about their marriage, Ellen would throw a temper tantrum, and Daniel, trying to make peace at any price for his daughter's sake, would just shut down and walk away.

"Daniel, Ellen's what I call a committed-commitment-phobic. She's married to you, but she wants to have her cake and eat it too. She's coming home with her body only, but her heart, soul, and mind seem to be somewhere else. Commitment-phobes always have to call all the shots. She's the master over you, and she manipulates you with every trick in the book to keep you under her thumb. You're going to have to approach the situation as her equal and expect to be treated as one. You can't continue to allow her to scream at you as if you're being a bad little boy questioning mommy. If you can't do this for your own sake, do it for your daughter's sake. Children relive the marriage they see before the age of five, because that's when their subconscious mind is forming. Do you like the example of marriage that you and your wife are showing her? Would you be happy or horrified if, in the future, your beloved daughter duplicated your marriage and sought out a liar and a cheater?"

"Of, course I'd be horrified!"

"Then do something about that. You're also going to have to address the pink elephant in the room, aka Larry, whether she wants to talk about what's really going on with him or not."

Three months later, when Daniel came back for another session, he told me that he had tried his best to talk with his wife, but she never gave him a straight answer, and for the most part, she just humored him. The final straw came when Ellen didn't come home one night, and yet, she didn't feel that she had to explain her whereabouts to Daniel. "You're not my father," was all she said.

At that point, Daniel saw the writing on the wall and filed for a divorce.

Ellen warned him, "You're going to live to regret that decision. I'm going to make your life hell."

True to her word on that one, Ellen did everything she could to make Daniel's life miserable. Throughout the divorce, I kept advising him to visualize divorce without drama and trauma. I told him to tell his daughter that she was not to get caught in the middle of this. He was advised to tell her, "When Mommy bad-mouths me, please don't defend me. Daddy is a big man and can defend himself."

The divorce proved to be a financial bloodbath for Daniel, but he had been enslaved to Ellen, and he had to buy his freedom. To this day he says, "It was the best money I ever spent."

A month after their divorce was finalized, Ellen moved in with Larry. A year later, he left her for a much younger woman, and Ellen found herself without a man and without a job. Ellen begged Daniel to take her back. She kept swearing to him that she had never been romantically involved with Larry until after they separated. Daniel couldn't help laughing when he heard that one.

The great news is that Daniel is now remarried to his Soul Mate, Jennifer, and they treat each other as two equals, showing his daughter, and their new son, Max, what real love looks like. As for Ellen—who cares!

Messages from the other side: During the first session that I had with Daniel, his grandfather on his mother's side channeled through me to tell Daniel that he had always been a good boy since the day he was born. At the mere mention of his grandfather, Daniel broke down in tears saying, "I always thought of my grandpa as my dad. After my parents' divorce, we went to live with him for a few years, and those were the happiest days of my life."

Daniel told me that his grandfather had passed away about five years ago, and that he missed him every day of his life.

"Daniel, your grandfather is saying that you always knew right from wrong and that you were a very bad liar! If you ever tried to lie your way out of situation, within a minute you would just break down and tell the truth, the whole truth, and nothing but the truth. He's also saying that he was so glad that you were never anything like your father. He's asking you to love yourself the way he loves you. He says that it's very painful for him to watch from above the situation between you and your wife. He says that he can't stand her, and that she's way too much like your lying, cheating father for his taste. That woman wouldn't know the truth if it bit her in the butt."

Daniel burst out laughing. "My grandpa always said that about my father, that he wouldn't know the truth if it bit him in the butt."

In the next session, Daniel told me how grateful he was to hear from his grandfather, and that he felt that his grandfather was with him a lot over the last few weeks. During that particular session, Ellen's grandmother on her mother's side came through. She had died when Ellen was seven, and she claimed that it was she who brought Ellen and Daniel together. She had hoped that if Ellen met a Soul Mate when she was fairly young, she would know how to love properly, and escape the family tradition of disastrous marriages. She told Daniel, "I didn't bring the two of you together so that she could break your heart. I give you my permission to do what you have to do to make things right for yourself and your daughter. In the meantime, I promise to try and pop some thoughts into Ellen's head that she is going to lose you, if she doesn't clean up her act."

Daniel told me that the one person that Ellen had truly loved unconditionally in this life was her grandmother and that when her grandmother died, Ellen felt alone and abandoned.

"Daniel, very few people maintain Soul Mate love over the long haul. One of the main reasons for people's inability to love properly is their deep, terrifying, primal fear of abandonment. Loving someone with your entire heart, soul, mind, and body, and having someone love you the same way back, still doesn't mean that this beloved person won't die on you and leave you all alone in your misery.

This fear of losing someone via death is why so many people systematically begin watering down love until it becomes a mediocre, more manageable emotion. This way, should their mate up and die on them, they can easily find another replacement in record time. If people drag love all the way down to a toxic level, well, who cares if this person dies? In fact, if it gets bad enough, these people might even kill each other! Before people can have a deep and lasting love, they have to overcome their fear of losing someone via the instrument of death."

Daniel looked at me as if a light had gone off in his head and a moment later said, "For the first time in my life, I understand Ellen. Her fear of loving someone who could die on her is so strong that she won't even allow our daughter into her heart."

I truly believe that both of these grandparents, delivering messages to Daniel from the other side, ultimately helped him find his way out of his toxic marriage.

The Four Kinds of People Who Inhabit the Earth

1. *The Great Enablers,* aka *The Donkey People,* aka *The Crap Takers,* who are good to a fault
2. *The Unfixables,* who are the bad to the bone *Self-Serving Narcissists*
3. *The Dr. Jekyll/Mr. Hyde-types,* "when they are good they are very, very good, and when they are bad they are horrid"
4. *The Enlightened Ones,* who know it's all good

Type One—*The Great Enablers*

The Good-to-a-Fault People are the real reason I sat down to write this book in the first place. Having spent way too many hours of my life writing, at this point, I really had no intention of writing another nonfiction book. But watching the good people suffer at the hands of *The Unfixables*, brought me to my knees far too many times for me to remain silent any longer. I call these *Good-to-a-Fault People "The Great Enablers."* They're also known as *The Donkey People,* because they're the workhorses of the world. They carry the workload at work and at home, and they appear to have very few needs of their own. Just give them a little water and a little hay, and they'll carry everyone's crosses, clean up everyone's messes, and pick up the tab as well. They're also known as *The Crap Takers.* They're so inherently good that they don't walk away when the crap hits their sandals; no, they wait until they're about to suffocate before they turn and walk away.

Key Traits That Characterize *The Great Enablers,* aka *The Donkey People,* aka *The Great Crap Takers*

1. They're good at playing "the rescuer" and "the victim" in the deadly triangle of behavior. They're not very good at playing "the persecutor."
2. They want everyone to like them.
3. They're loyal to a fault.
4. They tend to see the good in everyone.
5. Momentarily, they are capable of bringing out the best in everyone.
6. Because they tend to see the good in others, and momentarily bring out the best in others, they tend to get involved with the "Prince or Princess Who Becomes the Beast," both personally and professionally.
7. They forgive others too easily and too often.
8. They never forgive themselves for the slightest mistakes or transgressions.

9. They have a great need to "fix" or "rescue others." Believing that they can change others is their own brand of narcissism.

10. If they are ever in need of rescuing, and someone does appear to come on as "the rescuer," they remain loyal to this person indefinitely, even after time and time again, this person proves to be unworthy of such fidelity.

11. They're plagued with unearned and oftentimes nameless guilt because they somehow believe "*That it's all their fault.*"

12. They truly believe that their unconditional love can heal others.

13. They are unselfish to a fault and always put others first.

14. They make way too many excuses for abuse.

15. They feel bad when they have to walk away from someone, even when this person has betrayed them.

16. They're the peacemakers of the world, and they don't like to rock the boat. For the most part, they're people pleasers who make peace at any price.

17. Even if they know that the person they're with has cheated, lied, and abused other people, they can't believe that this person would do it to them. Believing that people won't do bad things to them is *The Great Enablers'* own brand of narcissism.

18. They can easily be manipulated by others because of all the above-stated traits.

Key Traits That Characterize *The Unfixables*

1. They can sometimes be classified as sociopaths or psychopaths, since they lack a conscience; or they

can just be your garden-variety type of manipulators, who always leave others feeling battered and abused.

2. They can come on very sweet and are often very charismatic.

3. They are highly manipulative.

4. Nothing is ever their fault.

5. They can play any role, "the victim," "the rescuer," or "the persecutor," but their Oscar performance usually goes to "the persecutor."

6. They never take responsibility for their actions.

7. They are pathological liars.

8. The truly sad fact is this: they believe their lies.

9. They are prone to addictions: drugs, alcohol, sex, gambling, spending, whatever!

10. They will, and quite often do, throw anyone and everyone under the bus, whenever it suits them.

11. They have mastered the art of guilting people into doing things for them.

12. They often come on as "the rescuer," only to victimize and persecute that person later on.

13. They're often engaged in fraudulent and illegal activities.

14. They will do whatever it takes to protect themselves, including stealing, maiming, or killing others.

15. They can come out on top because of their ruthlessness and ability to be con artists and convincing liars.

16. They can betray you with a kiss or sell you for a few pieces of silver.

17. They prey on *The Good-to-a-Fault People's* own brand of narcissism. Firstly, *The Great Enablers* believe that everything wrong in this world is somehow their fault; therefore, it's easy for *The Unfixables* to push their guilt buttons. Secondly, they use *The Great Enablers'* need to fix others as a weapon to get them to stick around in the false hopes that *The Unfixables* can change. Thirdly, *The Great Enablers* truly believe

that others will do unto them as they would do unto others, and that somehow makes them believe that they're immune to the *The Unfixables'* shenanigans. These three errors in *The Great Enablers'* thinking work to *The Unfixables'* advantage.

18. They're highly judgmental of others.

19. They're greedy and needy, and no amount of things or attention is ever enough.

20. They need constant adoration and praise.

21. It's all about how things look on the outside, and they don't pay attention to what's swept under the rug or stashed in the closet.

22. They'll wine and dine you when they need you, and later throw you under the bus, without missing a beat.

23. They have no sense of boundaries and will give you way too much information when it suits them, and leave out pertinent information when they feel like it.

24. They wouldn't know the truth if it bit them in the butt.

25. They'll deny the truth of something, even when the truth is staring them right in the face.

26. The difference between good people and bad people is simple: the good people know when they're doing something wrong, and the bad people are in total denial of their wrongdoings. For example, good people know that when they've had a hissy fit or temper tantrum they could have handled the situation better. Later on, when the dust settles, they try to make amends for these actions, and they honestly try never to repeat them again. As for *The Unfixables,* they couldn't care less whether they're actions are considered right or wrong, because in their viewpoint, the end justifies the means. They totally see the world through their self-serving lenses. These

are the kinds of people who aren't sorry for what they've done; they're just sorry that they got caught.

———⦿———

Remember this: **The Unfixables** *are people who you cannot fix, no way, no how. These people can only fix themselves. Unfortunately, this rarely happens!*

———⦿———

Key Traits That Characterize
The Dr Jekyll/Mr. Hyde-types

These people might be the hardest people of all to deal with, since we never know which way they will go.

1. They can sometimes play "the rescuer" role, but they're equally good at portraying "the persecutor" and "the victim" as well.
2. They can be good at times, when it suits them, but they're easily swayed by people and will take on the characteristics of others, good or bad, depending upon who they're currently associated with.
3. They're equally good at manipulating others, and they can be manipulated by others as well.
4. They can be the best of friends; they can be the worst of friends.
5. They're very fear-based people, and so their fears may make them do things they know in their heart of hearts aren't right.
6. They're selfish and greedy people, and this can lead them down the road to ruin.
7. When it comes to a love interest, money, or power, these people can turn on you on a dime.
8. When everything is going well, they can act in a morally correct manner, but when things aren't going

their way, they will do what they have to in order to get what they want.

9. They are highly narcissistic and tend to see the world through that self-serving lens.

Key Traits That Characterize *The Enlightened Ones*

1. Only a small percentage of people actually respond in appropriate ways to life with all its myriad of experiences on a consistent basis. ***The Enlightened Ones*** react realistically and strategically as they journey through their lives, because they have learned to see people for who they truly are and to see what is truly in front of their faces. They know how to respond to whatever life may toss their way, and they manage to do this while remaining calm, truthful, and assertive. On the other hand, a high percentage of people have a distorted vision of the world, viewing it with self-serving lenses, rose-colored glasses, or blinders on.

2. They have an unfaltering sense of integrity and a great need to seek truth. They're spiritual people, yet free from the constraints of dogma.

3. For the most part, they have liberated themselves from the powerful hold of the deadly triangle of behavior. They don't suffer from victim consciousness, since they know children are the only beings on this earth who can be victimized. They have no need to continually rescue others. They realize that people are entitled to a limited number of rescues: one get-out-of-jail-free card, one rehab, and one time that their lives become a sinking Titanic and they need some bailing out. After the three-strikes-they're-out, then ***The Enlightened Ones*** know to get out of

God's way and leave these people where they fall. They know how to teach others to fish, rather than to keep on fishing for them. They know if they've helped someone once that doesn't mean they have to carry that person on their backs for the rest of their lives. They have no need to carry other's crosses, since they realize that in life it's enough that they merely carry their own.

4. They don't play the role of "the persecutor," but they do know that justice must be done, and they do what they have to do to see that justice is carried out. They're peacemakers by nature, but they do know when to wage a war—when to see to it that people suffer the consequences of their actions, be it a lawsuit, jail time, or other fair and just punitive actions. They don't allow others to manipulate them. If someone says, "How could you put me in jail?" they know that it was that person's actions that landed him or her in jail; therefore, *The Enlightened Ones* walk away in peace.

5. *The Enlightened Ones* realize that they're messengers. They deliver messages of truth, tempered with kindness, and what people do with these messages is ultimately up to them. *The Enlightened Ones* don't take responsibility for anyone's actions but their own. They know that "it's all good" in the long run and that the outcome of a situation is not always up to them.

6. They're not manipulated by guilt, since they genuinely know that they're good people and that they would never intentionally hurt others. They always see clear to their intentions, and their intentions always serve everyone's higher good, including their own.

7. They don't stuff down anger, since they realize anger is a valid emotion when someone has betrayed them,

hurt them, stolen from them, cheated them, or lied to them. They believe in righteous anger, which is divine anger in action, and true justice for all.

What Kind of Person Are You Anyway and What Kind of People Are You Surrounded By?

Now that you have read the above traits of the four kinds of people on the planet, what kind of person do you think that you are?

Please take some time to think about the main people in your life, your significant other, your family members, coworkers, and friends, and try to figure out what kind of people they basically are.

This exercise in thinking is one of the first steps in ripping the blinders off. Once the rose-colored glasses come off, true sight begins.

The Great Enablers, The Unfixables, and the *Dr. Jekyll/Mr. Hyde-types* all have one thing in common: an inability to see reality.

The Enlightened Ones truly see the world for what it is.

———— ❦ ————

Remember: You can only see what your thoughts allow you to see. When you see what is truly before you, and when you stop practicing the art of denial, that is when true vision becomes possible.

———— ❦ ————

The Art of Manipulation

First, of all, let's define the word *manipulation*. Manipulation is the art of shrewdly controlling, managing, or influencing others, often using fraudulent, deceitful, or unfair methods, for one's own purpose or personal gain.

25

In terms of relationships, both personal and professional, manipulative people, either overtly or covertly, try to control or influence other people's thoughts, desires, feelings, or behaviors.

Although **Well-Meaning Narcissists** are not above the art of manipulation, they usually do it for what they believe to be the right reasons. We usually say about these kinds of people, "They meant well."

Self-Serving Narcissists are great manipulators of a different sort, and they're masters of deception. Just like magicians, these kinds of manipulators depend upon a lot of smoke and mirrors and tricks up their sleeves to achieve their desired outcome. They're Machiavellian in nature, and the end truly justifies the means. They'll use love or fear or both to control us, and are masters at reading other people's thoughts and body language, and figuring out which emotion and which tricks will work best on each person and in each different situation. The best manipulators are truly evil geniuses.

This book will help you see their tactics, techniques, and traps, and reveal the many masks they wear. Good manipulators are tenacious, cunning, intelligent, shrewd, and charming. They're also pathological liars, good actors, and chameleons, who change their colors to suit any situation.

The main reason people manipulate is to gain power and control. As you read this chapter, I want you to think of the people in your life who have used manipulation to disempower you. I also want you to be brutally honest with yourself and acknowledge if and when you've been guilty of manipulating others to gain control over them. Vow from this day forward to speak your truths without fear or worry of outcome. Relinquish and extinguish the control freak in you. It's not your job to save everyone, rescue everyone, fix every situation, and to play God. Follow your heart and higher consciousness, and leave the rest in the hands of karma and go in peace.

Manipulation is a very fear-based way of thinking, and fear is one of the weapons manipulators use to control others. They use love, and the fear of the loss of their love, to control others as well.

In dealing with manipulators, we must act calmly and strategically. This gives us time to come up with a methodology and a game plan in which we can best protect ourselves from the very real damage and potential damage that these kinds of people can inflict on our lives.

One warning: manipulators are like viruses. Just when we think we're immune to them, they mutate.

The Manipulators' Bottomless Bag of Tricks

1. **Power Plays**—They're great at bullying others with threats of physical violence or with harsh and menacing words. They're masters of using veiled and not-so-veiled threats. Pushing people's fear of abandonment buttons is a favorite tactic, and they will use any form of intimidation they can think of to get us to do what they want.

2. **Playing "The Rescuer" in the Deadly Triangle of Behavior**—They love playing the knight in shining armor or the mommy/daddy figure that comes and scrapes us off the floor and sweeps us off our feet. They love making us feel that we're forever indebted to them.

3. **Shaming, Blaming, and Guilting Us to Death**—Manipulators never take responsibility for their actions and are masters at turning the table around and somehow making us feel that everything is all our fault. They will use guilt-arousing expressions such as: "This is how you thank me for all I have done?" Or, "if your father were alive, you'd never be

talking to me this way." Or, "don't come crying to me when things don't turn out the way you wanted."

How Do We Feel When We're in the Midst of an Ace Manipulator?

Let's put it this way—it never feels good! We feel beaten, broken, blamed, and shamed into doing things that we really don't want to do. Manipulators have a way of making us feel anxious, cornered, helpless, needy, paranoid, frustrated, angry, confused, dazed, battle fatigued, and, most of all, guilt ridden. All manipulators are "Energy Vampires." They'll take all and give nothing, and suck you dry and walk away without ever looking back. After dealing with them, we feel exhausted and drained. We end up saying and doing things that we really don't want to. Eventually, manipulators leave us feeling angry, depressed, and mad as hell, not so much at them, but at ourselves for allowing them to take advantage of us, time and time again.

I want you to keep one thing in mind. If you're a good person who has never intentionally hurt anyone in your entire life, then why should anyone ever make you feel guilty? I have an expression that I love to use, and I think you will, too: "*You lost me at the guilt.*" Say it, mean it, and then walk away in peace.

The Different Kinds of Manipulators

As you look over the following list of the different kinds of manipulators there are, notice how archetypal in character the roles these people portray actually are—for instance, the Con Artist, the Judge, and the Prince and the Princess. These people's manipulations work on us because they hit us in our weak spots— our subconscious minds. By the time our conscious minds catch up with things, the manipulators have already left us in the dust.

It's My Way or No Way

These are the control freaks. If they happen to be our parents, lovers, or bosses, we're in for a whammy. They control us in many ways, but badgering, nagging, whining, screaming, and raging are some of the techniques they're fond of. The silent treatment, threats, and blackmail are also part of their arsenals. They're good at pushing others' fear-of-abandonment buttons, and this is another way that they get people to see things their way. They will rain on your parade; they are geniuses in knowing what you might fear in any situation, and they're sure to tell you everything that can and will go wrong should you decide to do something that they don't want you to do.

They're also good at saying "I told you so," and will remind us of all the things that ever went wrong when we didn't listen to them.

They will guilt us into doing things or not doing them, and they'll be sure to let us know that, should things go wrong, "Don't come crying to me."

They're not above lying or leaving out facts, because they're true Machiavellians who believe the end justifies the means, and since they know best—anything goes.

I Am Smarter or More Gifted Than Anyone Else

These people can be the great intellectual minds of the world, the writers, entertainers, politicians, athletes, artists, and the so-called geniuses. They think that they're smarter or more gifted than everyone else; therefore, they don't have to play by the rules.

The paparazzi have a field day following the antics of these "chosen" ones. Reality TV has brought us a whole lot of nobodies who think they're "somebodies." Their often outlandish behaviors further serve to reinforce their right to do whatever it is they want to, and they're shocked when they're asked to account for their behaviors.

They can also just be plain old delusional or psychopathological, or the megalomaniacs of the world, who really and truly believe that they're the "Entitled Ones."

The "Stupidvisor"

Unfortunately, all of us have encountered these kinds of manipulators throughout our lifetimes, whether at home, school, work, or at play. These people truly believe they know how to do everything best; meanwhile, in reality, they don't know the first thing about anything. They sit on the sidelines shouting to others what they could have and should have done better, and what they themselves would have done better had they been out there on the playing field instead.

They're truly lazy and incompetent people, and they've never done an ounce of real work in their lifetimes, but they're really good at manipulating others to do their work for them. Think of Mark Twain's character, Tom Sawyer, and the whitewashing-the-fence episode. Tom manipulated the other boys into thinking that whitewashing the fence wasn't work at all, but great fun and a great privilege to have been chosen to do. Before long, the neighborhood boys started handing over their worldly goods to him, just for the opportunity to try their hand at whitewashing the fence.

Meanwhile, Tom got to sit back and watch the show, ruminating on the odd nature of human beings and on how easily you can make others covet things—simply by making those things seem difficult to attain.

It's Always All about *Me*

When these ace manipulators talk, it sounds like, *"It's about me, myself, and I. Oh, that's enough about me talking about me.*

What do you think about me?" They're so self-absorbed and self-centered that they're oblivious to the needs and wants of others.

They're the supreme Energy Vampires of the world, and they take all and give nothing. They're the *"what-have-you-do-ne-for-me-lately types."* As long as they need you, or you're giving them what they want, they'll be your best friends. If you start asking for something in return, they will drop you like a hot potato and find some other sucker to be their slave.

Sweeter Than Honey: They Butter Us Up and Then Eat Us Alive

They don't use fear to get their way. They use love. They make us feel good about ourselves. They're filled with compliments about how great and competent we are. They're oh so sweet as they laugh about how inept and incompetent they are— as if they can't even screw in a light bulb—and the next thing we know, we're doing it for them! Later on, we're left wondering, *who's the dumb one, them or us?*

These are the "crazy-like-a-fox" manipulators. With these people, we don't usually see it coming, and it might even take us quite some time to figure out what they're up to. They use a subtle form of guilt-tripping, in which we would feel *bad* if we didn't do what they wanted or buy whatever wares they were selling.

In terms of archetypes, the sweet manipulators are the flirts, the femme fatales, the damsels in distress, and the Peter Pan types.

The Dictators

The Dictators are the consummate bullies of the world. Bullying behaviors come in many forms, but most bullies set out to break us psychologically. There are basically four types of bullying: physical, emotional, psychological, and verbal. Most bullies use a combination of all four tactics to break down their victims. Bullies need power and use and abuse others to make themselves feel in control and better about themselves. Whether the threat is to our bodies, hearts, minds, or souls doesn't really matter; we just feel intimidated by these people.

Bullies never play fair or by any rules but their own. They're cowards and often covertly bully others. The newest breed of bullies are the cyber-bullies, posting nasty and threatening comments on the Internet—anonymously of course, since they don't have the courage to put their names where their mouths are.

Bullies scare us by their very irrational natures. Many of them are loose cannons with rage issues. They never fight fair or go an eye for an eye. No, they go after both of your eyes, your left arm, your right leg, and your firstborn as well.

Think: Hitler, Mussolini, and Stalin, just to name a few of the top bullies in recent times.

After All I Did for You—The Guilt Trippers

We're all familiar with this type of manipulation. Mothers are notorious guilt trippers. Of course, these mothers feel justified in using their guilt tactics to control their children; after all, they're only doing it for their children's own good, and mother knows best.

Children are also masters of pushing their parents' guilt buttons. If you're the kind of person who didn't have good parents, you'll probably bend over backward in an attempt to be a great parent. Your children know this, and they'll always find a way to guilt you into doing what they want you to do. In the great scheme of things, all we really need to be is "good enough" parents. So, I give you permission to stop trying to be the world's best one. You're not responsible for all of your children's bad choices. Teach them to take what they want, but to pay for it. At times, you might just have to leave them where they fall, while praying that they don't fall too hard. If you keep carrying your children's crosses and cleaning up their messes, you'll only teach them to keep on being irresponsible and to keep passing the buck.

The Rewriters of History—The Perennial Victims

These manipulators are famous for their selective memories. They see the world through their self-serving, narcissistic lenses, and really believe that it happened the way they said it happened. Consequently, they truly believe nothing is ever their fault. They play the victim role very well and never take any responsibility for the mess their lives are in. They blame everything on their parents, the economy, the latest president of the United States, you, and just about anyone else they can think of!

This group also includes the Deniers. They didn't see it happen, and so it never happened. The Deniers are the reason so much evil goes unpunished. They deny the existence of evil; therefore, it doesn't exist. If they hide their heads in the sand and don't see what's going on right under their noses, then they don't have to deal with any crimes or crimes against humanity that come their way.

The Deniers will stand their ground, twisting and turning the truth to no end, swearing, "It wasn't me," and adamantly swearing that they didn't do something they were accused of. Lance Armstrong, former professional cyclist, practiced this form of manipulation for a long time, angrily denying allegations of doping, only to reveal the truth on national television to Oprah. This is another form of manipulation—let me tell you a little bit of truth and now you have to forgive me. Narcissists crave attention. Grandstanding, on national television to confess sins best left to the confessional or to more private ways of revelations, is just another form of mass manipulation.

We can cite Anthony Weiner, the former US representative from New York's Ninth Congressional District who resigned from Congress in June 2011 after the whole sexting scandal came to light, as another example of a Denier. When his sexting shenanigans first surfaced in 2011, he adamantly denied and lied his way right out of Congress. In 2013, he resurfaced as a New York City mayoral hopeful. It didn't take long for a new cyber mistress, Sydney Leathers, to come forth with more tales of textual abuse. We can call this kind of denial of sexual wrongdoing *Pulling a Weiner.*

The Self-Anointed Judge and Jury of Everyone

These kinds of manipulators judge everybody all the time, and they believe that whatever group they belong to—the country club, country, political party, religion, or race—is the superior and righteous one. They manipulate others by making them feel inferior, and they exert an inordinate amount of energy in an effort to convince others that their own thoughts and opinions are wrong. These kinds of manipulators are always trying to recruit others to join their cause or organization.

These people think that they're perfect; therefore, nothing that ever goes wrong is their fault.

Oftentimes the very flag they're waving and the cause they're fighting for are just ruses to throw us off the track, so that we don't see what these self-righteous people are truly up to.

We can cite former New York Governor Eliot Spitzer as a prime example of this kind of manipulation. Although he was famous for his moralistic crusade against prostitution and often took a holier-than-thou approach to this topic, his political career went crashing down when news surfaced that he had used an escort service and spent thousands of dollars on a high-end prostitute. Of course, these kinds of manipulators have no shame and no guilt and will always try to bask in the limelight time and time again.

If someone is guilty of denying his or her own sexual misconduct, but judges others, we can call this kind of behavior *Pulling a Spitzer-Weiner.*

Feigning Weakness or Illness So That You'll Come Rescue Me

These people play the psychological game of wooden leg and make us all feel that they can't live without us. Somehow, they always get someone to carry their crosses and clean up their messes. They use their supposed helplessness or illness to keep others in line, and they always have the upper hand in relationships. They are the "woe-with-me" types who inevitably will outlive us all.

The Rage-Aholic

We shut up and do what these lunatics want, because we don't want to be in the range of their target. They have temper tantrums and won't let anyone get a word in one way or another. We usually give in to them, because it's easier to do that than to bear witness to one of their meltdowns. We tend to make a lot of excuses for these people's abuses. We feel sorry for them because they've had hard childhoods, or we buy into the labels—that they have some kind of chemical imbalance or mental illness that they just can't control. Ironically, they can clean up their acts and look normal when they want to, another version of crazy like a fox.

Jake LaMotta, the Italian-American retired professional boxer who was the subject of the highly acclaimed Martin Scorsese film, *Raging Bull,* is a good example of a rage-aholic. This kind of rage is certainly handy in the ring, and it helped him to mass-manipulate his fans and the boxing world to rally in his corner during his matches; however, using these same tactics in his private life, in an effort to control others, didn't always result in a standing ovation.

The Halo Effect

These manipulators are the great bullshit artists of the world. They're excellent listeners when they first meet us. Systematically, over a short period of time, they manage to parrot back to us everything we previously professed to want and believe, giving us the illusion that they think just like us. You know the type. We all know the type!

One of my clients, Joyce, went on a first date with Roy, a man she had met on an Internet dating site. She had told him that her first husband had cheated on her, and Roy said, "I've never cheated on a woman." Over the course of the next few dates, he would always work in a story about someone who cheated and how much he hated that. Joyce was in seventh heaven. Finally, she had found a man who thought like her and who had her same value system.

After a year of dating, she went to the gynecologist and was shocked to learn she had chlamydia. When she confronted Roy about this, he insisted the infection wasn't from him and that she must have contracted it from her cheating ex-husband. A month later, when Roy was sick with a cold and napping, she heard his cell phone ring four times in a row. She didn't want to wake him, but just in case it was an emergency or some work-related urgent matter, she picked up. She couldn't believe what she heard: a woman frantically blabbering, "I can't meet you tomorrow. My husband's on to us." When Joyce confronted Roy about what she had just heard, he turned everything around, stating, "You had no right to answer my phone, bitch."

The Halo Effect manipulators do great on job interviews. They convince the interviewers that they know how to do everything. Once on the job, that halo effect lasts for a while, until someone catches on that these people don't know how to do anything, let alone everything.

The Drama Kings and Queens

These people are great at convincing us that the sky is falling. They always need rescuing, always need to be the center of attention, and always keep us in a state of chaos. They love to stir up the pot and cause conflict, and they love adding fuel to the fire.

They're always the victims of someone or something. In talking with them, you hear a lot of me, myself, and I, and it's all your fault or somebody else's fault that their lives are a mess.

In order for things to play out, they need to recruit other players in their dramas, and they are very good at sucking people in.

One of my clients, Jane, was married to a Drama King named Harry. She dreaded going out in public with him. Everything always seemed to go wrong, no matter where Harry went. For example, if they went to a restaurant, he would create a scene about the food not being right. In the movie theater, somebody would rub him the wrong way, and a fight would ensue. Wherever Harry went, a riot followed.

When Jane went to divorce Harry, you can only imagine the drama that took place in the divorce court. For his performance, Harry really should have earned an Oscar!

It's All Your Fault Because You Didn't Fix Me!

These manipulators are very adept at knowing the fatal flaws in *The Good-to-a-Fault People*. *The Great Enablers* somehow feel that it's their job to fix everyone and rescue everyone. *Now doesn't that sound like a very narcissistic trait?* Think about it. Believing that it's your job to solve everybody's problems, clean up everybody's messes, and carry their crosses sounds an awful lot like you're playing God. God doesn't know how to fix people either, but God does keep giving people one wake-up call after another in the hope that something will change. Ultimately, it's a freewill universe, and I can't stress this enough—manipulative people only wake up when the gun is at their heads. As soon as things return to normal, the manipulators start their deceptive games all over again.

Get over your need to fix people, and learn to leave them where they fall. Stop enabling, cradling, and believing that you were born to fix the world. Fixing yourself is a hard enough task.

The Prince and Princess Who Become the Beast

We all know the story of *Beauty and the Beast*. The Disney version is probably the one we all know best. But come on…we all know the Beast—the hard-core drug addict, serial cheater, pathological liar, wife-beating psychopath—you get the drift—rarely becomes the Prince or Princess, no matter how many chances or how much therapy this person receives. (Yes, miracles do happen, when and if the Beast earns one!)

However, we have all seen, way too often, the Prince or Princess Who Becomes the Beast. These people have mastered the art of listening to us when they first meet us, and spewing back almost verbatim what we've told them, giving us the illusion that they think and act just like us. In the beginning, they can't work hard enough, or help us enough, or be there enough for us. In fact, they often come into our lives when we are at a moment of weakness, when we need some rescuing. For instance, right around the time we've just buried a loved one, or when we've just gone through a bad divorce or been laid off. They help us once, and then for the rest of our lives we find ourselves rescuing them.

These people can clean themselves up when and if they need to, and they can fool an awful lot of people. It's only after we get really involved with them, marry them, or start a business with them that their true colors show. We're usually shocked to realize that they can't do anything that they said they could, or that they're addicts, or in debt. They are the true con artists who can break the bank and your heart, leaving you to wonder—*what the hell happened?*

The Crazy Like a Fox

These kinds of manipulators master many of the other manipulation techniques. Their main personality trait is that they never do anything that they don't want to do. They often feign illness and claim to be mentally ill or disabled; therefore, they can't work, but they manage to be able to do just about anything else—if they feel like it.

They're always looking for another sucker who will feel sorry for them.

They sucker people in with their "woe is me" tales and will use any situation to get their ways.

They're always telling us how honest they are while they're robbing us blind. They tell us they have no money, so we pay for everything, only to later learn that they have all kinds of money stashed away.

A rule of thumb with the crazy-like-a-fox crowd goes as follows: if they tell you they have no money, you can bet your bottom dollar that they've got millions; conversely, if they tell you that they've got millions, you can bank on the fact that they don't even have a pot to piss in!

The Hypnotists

These are the master manipulators. They're charismatic, charming, and convincing. They can sweet-talk us, brainwash us, and get us to follow them anywhere. They have intense personalities, and people are naturally drawn to them.

When the Hypnotists happen to be physically attractive as well, they're even more dangerous. Their good looks further aid them in their keen ability to keep people in a trance-like state. They are Svengali-like in the way they can command, control, and convince their victims that they can't live without them. They're smooth talkers, and later on, we're left wondering, *why did we go along with them in the first place?*

They draw people to them like magnets and use and abuse others without the least bit of conscience. If they happen to be in the limelight—a celebrity or public personality—we can find ourselves working for them for no money, being their gofer, covering up for them, and cleaning up their messes.

The hypnotic personalities are highly effective in seducing their prey and then walking away, without ever looking back.

Dumb and Dumber

These people want us to think that they're too dumb to know how to do anything. They don't want to learn, even if you're willing to teach them. If you ask them to do something, they usually screw it up badly, ensuring that you will never ask them for help again.

Feigning ignorance allows them to avoid responsibility, to be the ones who never have to pitch in and help or step up to the plate.

By playing dumb, they get others to do everything for them.

By playing dumb, they never have to make a decision; therefore, no one can ever put the blame on them.

People can also play dumb as a way to gather information from us. They get us to reveal things to them because they keep asking a lot of dumb-sounding questions, and before we know it, we're squealing like pigs and revealing way too much information.

They also like to act as if they're too dumb to know what's going on, all the while gathering up all kinds of information to use against others at a later time.

The Count and Countess

These people always manage to have everyone waiting on them hand and foot. They're too good to clean up a mess, and they expect others to clean up after them. They like the best of everything, but don't think they have to work for it. They have a sense of entitlement and truly believe they're special. They don't think that they should have to follow the rules that others follow. They're impatient and angry when they have to wait in line, and they treat everyone like hired help.

They expect and demand special treatment. If they're our children, they expect us to buy them whatever they want and to bail them out whenever they get in trouble. These kinds of children let us know that we shouldn't expect to get anything in return from them, except the privilege of being their parents.

If the Count and Countess happen to be our parents, who did little or nothing for us when we were growing up, they will nonetheless still expect us to sacrifice all, and even go into financial ruin, just to take care of them when they're dying; and they're usually on their deathbeds for what seems like an eternity to those of us who have to be around to answer their every beck and call.

The Holier Than Thou

They're an awful lot like the Self-Anointed Judge and Jury manipulators, but these people hide behind their religion and sit in judgment of others who don't follow their beliefs. They truly feel that those individuals who follow their faith are the chosen ones. They have a sense of self-righteousness and display an air of moral superiority. These people can hide behind their religion and judge everyone else's behavior by the rules of their game and their interpretation of dogma—in other words, "The World According to Me, Myself, and I."

Born-again religious zealots bring the judging of others to a whole new level. They obsessively try to convert others to their ways, and use guilt as one of their most lethal weapons. They will guilt their children into not marrying the love of their lives, if this person is of a different faith or belief system. They love conditionally and use threats of withdrawal of that love to control others.

They also use the fear of God to scare the bejesus out of us! Heaven help us when we encounter these manipulators!

The Devil Made Me Do It

These people are the kings and queens of convincing others that something possessed them or made them do something. They don't know why they had the affair and use "the devil made me do it" excuse to get their mates to forgive them.

It wasn't me, but the drugs or alcohol talking. They never take responsibility for their own reckless impulses and desires. They blame things on their friends or others and make us believe that they have seen the light, but time and time again, they will disappoint us.

Relegating responsibility to an outside force, demonic or otherwise, allows these people to avoid taking full responsibility for their less-than-stellar behaviors.

Look at What You Made Me Do

These people twist and turn things so much that somehow, no matter what they do, it wasn't their fault. You drove them to drink with your nagging. You made them hit you by questioning them.

If you make a statement or take a stand, somehow these fact-twisting people can and will use that against you.

Physically and emotionally abusive manipulators use this technique quite often. They're very good at convincing **The Great Enablers** that it truly was their fault, and this allows them to get away with murder!

The Bad Childhood

Nothing these people do is ever their fault. They blame everything on Mommy and Daddy. No matter how old they get, it doesn't matter—it's still their parents' fault. Because they've had abusive childhoods, they think that everyone should feel sorry for them. They truly believe that we should excuse today's bad behaviors, because they had it bad back in the day.

News flash: having an abusive childhood doesn't give anyone the right or a license to hurt others. There's a point where you just have to tell these people to knock it off, grow up, and get over it!

Charlatans, Tricksters, and Con Men

These are the "Madoffs" of the world, the snake oil salesmen, and the psychics who claim that you have a curse on you, or that they can bring back your lost love—for a whole lot of green, that is. These people will sell you the Brooklyn Bridge, the fountain of youth, or the keys to the kingdom. You can find them on Wall Street, in churches and temples, on Madison Avenue, in your neighborhood, and in your own backyard.

The Life of the Party

Everything is a joke to these manipulators. They have a joke for every occasion and then some. They're the masters of gallows humor—the humor that hangs, since this kind of black humor continually makes light of life-threatening, disastrous, or terrifying scenarios. If they're told by a doctor that if they don't stop drinking, they'll die, they'll joke, "What a way to go," or "Too bad I'll be too dead to drink at my own wake!" They laugh about their drunkenness or their addictions, and no matter how bad things are, life is but a joke to them.

They make us feel totally uncool if we don't want to play hooky or ditch a family obligation. They're often highly charismatic, and at first we might even buy into their laissez-faire attitude, wishing that we could be more like them and just throw caution to the wind. Sometimes, we even buy into their life-is-a-joke mentality, but later on, when we watch our finances and everything else around us sinking faster than the Titanic, we come to realize that we were charmed right into the poorhouse.

What You Don't Know Won't Hurt You

These are the kinds of people who lie by omission. They're adept at withholding large chunks of truth. They've mastered the art of being vague. When you ask them a direct question, they never give you a straight answer. Often, they just don't answer the question at all. They just switch the topic in record time.

One of my clients, Jessica, felt sure that her new boyfriend was loyal to her. But when I asked her if she'd had the talk with him about being exclusive, she said, "No, but he implied it." I told her, "That's not good enough. *Assuming* someone isn't sleeping with other people, doesn't mean that they aren't." Six months later, Jessica found out that she had a wicked case of gonorrhea. When she confronted her boyfriend, he claimed that she must have given it to him! When she told him that that was impossible, since he was the first man she had been with in over five years, he called her "A big, fat liar"!

With these kinds of manipulators, you have to learn to take matters in your hands by asking the questions that need answering. You can be sure they're lying about something when they won't answer you straight. It's up to you to investigate further, and see for yourself what this person is up to. Hiding your head in the sand about what your partner is doing doesn't mean that you can't get venereal disease, and ignoring the pink elephant in the room always comes back to bite you in the ass.

I'll Gladly Pay You Tuesday for a Hamburger Today

Like Wimpy, the harmless mooch from the cartoon *Popeye,* we all encounter people who mean well, but who never actually do what they say they will.

They're always borrowing something from us, usually money, and they promise to do all kinds of things for us in return, but never get them done. When these people are our neighbors or friends, they can be annoying and get on our nerves with all their borrowing and never paying back; but when these people happen to be our children, spouses, or employees, their laziness or spending habits can be much more than just annoying: they can land us in the poorhouse in no time!

Summing Things Up

There are countless other types of manipulators, and I'm sure that you can add a few other kinds of manipulations people have pulled on you to this list as well.

Let me state this once again: manipulators are like viruses. Just when we think we are immune to them, they mutate, and attack us once again!

———

Remember: most manipulators shift the game around, to throw you off the track and catch you off guard.

———

Strategies for Dealing with Manipulators: Learning to Outfox the Fox

1. You tell them what they want to hear—yeah, yeah, yeah, sure, and then you do what you want.
2. Turn the tables and show them how it feels to be manipulated and used.
3. You can guilt them back.
4. Run for the hills and don't look back!
5. Heal your own issues and overcome your own fears. Manipulators are geniuses at figuring out our weaknesses and our fears. They push all our fear buttons, and this is how they work their way into our lives. Heal yourself so that there are no cracks in your consciousness where these worms can wiggle their way into your life.
6. Keep reading this book for all kinds of insights into dealing with the manipulators of the world.
7. The most important weapon you have in your arsenal is your gut. Learn to trust your gut. If your inner

voice, your intuition, tells you someone is lying to you, then know that they are. If your gut tells you that they're manipulating you—then follow your instincts and respond in any of the above ways, but do not allow them to convince you to do what you do not want to do.

The New Golden Rule: If you aren't quite sure how to respond to a particular person or situation, I want you to filter it through the following lens: if someone did this exact thing to your son or daughter or to any person you love and protect as your own, would you tell this person to turn the other cheek or to sue the bastard? Whatever you would tell this beloved person to do in this particular situation is what you're to tell yourself to do.

Donna, *The Great Enabler,* Gets Conned Again by Eddie, *The Unfixable*

Donna first met Eddie back in 1972. Donna was an "A" student at an all girls' Catholic High School. She was the youngest of five children and was extremely shy around everyone, except the members of her immediate family.

The summer before her senior year, Donna got a lifeguard job at the local public pool. She never forgot the first time she laid eyes on Eddie. The temperature was soaring that July afternoon, and her heart skipped a beat when he walked over to her lifeguard stand, handed her an ice-cold lemonade, and said, "I didn't think things could get any hotter around here, but then I saw you." Donna remembered hearing Roberta Flack's hit "The First Time Ever I Saw Your Face" playing in the background on the radio, and she felt as if she were living out a scene from some romantic summer movie.

Over the next few weeks, Eddie, who was the manager of the pool's food concession, would always make a point to bring her something to eat or drink and hang around for a few minutes to talk with her. He told her that he had just turned nineteen, and Donna was amazed that he was the first guy, besides her brother, that she had ever felt comfortable around.

It wasn't just Donna who adored Eddie; everyone at the pool thought he was the greatest guy on earth, because if someone didn't have any money that day, well, that was no problem for Eddie, because he'd just give you something on the house. A month later, when Eddie got fired for this behavior, everyone, including Donna, felt really sorry for him; after all, he was just being nice.

After he got fired, Eddie was really bummed out. He told Donna that he had to drop out of school in his senior year because his alcoholic father had landed in jail for a hit-and-run accident, and he needed to support his mom and two brothers. Donna thought he was a saint. Eddie kept telling her how hard he was looking for work, and back in the day, it never dawned on Donna that he still spent most of his time hanging around the poolside the rest of that summer.

Donna's brother said, "Donna, the guy doesn't want to work. When he ran the concession, he spent most of his time yapping to everybody while all the young kids worked their tails off cooking and cleaning. He's a bum!" Donna, who usually worshipped the ground her brother walked on, told him that he was way off base about Eddie and that any further discussions about Eddie were off-limits from now on.

Toward the end of August, Donna and Eddie started dating, and Donna kept telling everyone how this was the best summer of her life. On Labor Day, Eddie came to her annual family barbeque to meet the rest of her family. Donna was in seventh heaven as she sat in the kitchen helping her mother, all the while gazing out the big picture window at Eddie, who was in her backyard shooting hoops with her father and brother.

Four decades later, Donna's blue eyes filled with tears as she told me the sad story of how her first love ended that Labor Day. She said, "I was just putting the mayonnaise in the potato salad when the phone rang. I can still remember that call as clear as if it happened yesterday." When Donna picked up the receiver, she heard a baby screaming in the background, and a young woman said, "Eddie probably forgot to mention me, but I'm his wife, Annie. After he finishes screwing you, could you ask him to pick up some diapers? His newborn son has been crapping all day. It looks like little Eddie's gonna turn out to be a big shithead just like his father."

The only things Donna remembers about her senior year was that she was so depressed that she almost didn't graduate, and on the night of her prom, she stayed in her room crying her eyes out.

Forty years later, in August of 2012, Eddie asked Donna to be his Facebook friend. Donna had recently divorced her husband of thirty years because she had gotten tired of being told by him 24-7 what she could or couldn't do. Besides acting as if he owned her, Donna's husband was also verbally abusive and told her on a daily basis, "Who'd ever want you? You're fat and bad in bed." Both of her parents, who were staunch Catholics, had passed away that year, and now she felt free to leave her husband. When she had tried to leave him back in 2001, both of her parents had insisted, "You made a vow till death do you part; now go back to your husband." Donna, always the dutiful daughter, of course, had honored her parents' wishes.

Her two grown children had recently moved out of the sprawling suburban south shore Long Island home that she had kept in the divorce settlement, and Donna began feeling lonely. Finally she felt that it was time for her to start dating. The online dating services she had signed up for were proving to be a disaster, though. She said, "They were all sex addicts who just wanted to get in my pants and run. I was so depressed thinking that I was going to spend the rest of my life alone, and then Eddie friended me on Facebook, and I thought it was pure kismet."

Donna and Eddie started messaging back and forth. He apologized for being such an ass when he was younger, and told her that his son was almost forty now and living in Texas. He told her that he had been divorced from Annie for more than thirty years, and that he had just buried his son-of-a-bitch father.

About two weeks after the messaging started, Eddie asked Donna out on a date. From the moment she saw him again, Donna felt that same sense of ease with him that she had felt four decades before. Eddie told her, "You were the love of my life. Annie got herself knocked up, and I stepped up to the plate and did what was right, but I never loved her. There wasn't a day that passed that I didn't think of you."

On Labor Day of 2012, forty years after the infamous Annie phone call, Donna took Eddie to another family barbeque, this one hosted by her daughter, Ashley. Something about Eddie didn't ring true to Ashley, and as a NYPD detective, she always trusted her gut instincts. She said nothing at the time, but told herself to check him out.

After the barbeque, Eddie asked if he could spend the night. Donna recalled, "The first time we made love, Eddie said that he dreamed of this moment all of his life, and that I was more beautiful than he'd ever remembered, and that I satisfied him more than any women ever had." After all the years of hearing her ex-husband say how fat and bad in bed she was, these words melted her heart. Donna told him that she wanted to take things slowly, and Eddie said, "Your wish is my command."

In October of 2012, when Hurricane Sandy hit Long Island with a fury, Donna was shocked when Eddie landed on her doorstep. He said that his house in Riverhead had been destroyed by the storm, and he was wondering if he could stay—just for a few days. Donna, always the Good Samaritan, and feeling eternally grateful that her beloved home had been spared the scourge of water and wind that had destroyed so many of her nearby neighbors houses, let him move in.

A few days turned into a few months, and never once did Eddie offer Donna any money or mention that he was working on getting his house fixed. He claimed that he was waiting for the insurance money to come through, complained about all the red tape and the incompetence of people nowadays, and said he was just trying to be patient and not get a heart attack over it all. He said that he'd had some job or another with a friend of his, but that the business got ruined in the storm. He always told her, "Not to worry. The business will be up and running soon."

Eddie never seemed to leave the house much, and Donna's gut began telling her that something wasn't kosher. But she just ignored her instincts, telling herself that she was just being paranoid, and Eddie just needed some time to get back on his feet.

Eight months after Eddie had moved in, Donna came to me for a session to get some insight into the situation and some guidance on what she should do about it. She was really upset, saying, "I don't know how to get him out of my house." She then explained that her daughter, Ashley, had done some digging and found out that Eddie had been in and out of jail most of his adult life for offenses that ranged from driving under the influence to petty larceny. At first Eddie denied ever having been arrested, but recanted when Donna Googled his name right in front of him and information about a whole host of arrests appeared. Eddie then told her a litany of reasons why things weren't as they appeared. "I took the rap for my father that time," and "My friend didn't tell me that I was delivering drugs. I thought I was just delivering packages," and "I was taking Vicodin for my back pain when the cops pulled me over. I was on my way to work, and I could barely walk, the pain was so bad. I had a prescription for it and everything."

Donna, always a sucker for a sob story, found herself feeling sorry for him. She did tell him that he had a month to find another place, but that was already two months ago, and he was still living in her house.

I asked her, "What are you getting out of this arrangement?"

"Nothing, really. We stopped having sex right after he moved in. He had one excuse after another why. I thought maybe he was suffering from posttraumatic stress disorder from the hurricane and left him alone. I guess I just thought maybe things would get better. The final straw for me came yesterday, when my daughter told me that Eddie had no house in Riverhead that was destroyed by the storm. She found out that he had just gotten out of Suffolk County Jail in Riverhead the day that he Facebooked me."

I told her that she was guilty of making excuses for his abuse, and that she needed to stop giving him the benefit of the doubt. He was a liar and a manipulator forty years ago, and he hadn't changed one bit since. I told her over and over again that he wasn't her responsibility and that he wasn't her cross to carry. I also told her to pop in on him one day on her lunch break and find out what he does all day holed up in her home. "All I know is that he is always in front of his laptop when I get home," Donna said.

The first thing she discovered when she walked in on Eddie was that he was a porn addict. He was in the shower, but had left his computer open. Donna checked his browsing history, and it was filled with porn sites and online dating sites. "No wonder he's got nothing left for me," Donna remembered saying to herself. When she confronted him about his latest activities, he screamed at her, "You have no right to spy on me. You're damn right I'm moving out. You act like you're my mother the way you check up on me and nag at me." Donna wondered if she really had driven him away with her behavior, and she told him he could stay as long as he needed.

When she came to me the following month for some more guidance into the situation, I had to tell her that he was pushing her guilt buttons, twisting and turning the truth until he managed to turn the tables on her. I also told her that he was judging her to be the bad guy. All of his manipulations and judgments, combined with his porn addiction, made the prognosis of him ever changing slim to none. I told her that Eddie was one of **The Unfixables** and that she was being one of **The Great Enablers.**

Still, it took Donna a few more months to kick Eddie out. He kept telling her he was looking for a place, and one day he said that he had to go out of town on business, and even though Donna thought it sounded more like he had monkey business on the agenda, she didn't question him much.

The final straw came when he returned two days later. When he went to take a shower that night, he left his cell phone on the bed. Normally, he always locked his phone, but this time he must have forgotten to do so and Donna heard a text message come in. When she picked up his cell phone, she read a text he had written to another woman: "Yesterday was the best sex of my life. Suzie, I can't stop thinking about you…" Suzie's answer was, "Ditto. I've got a closet and dresser emptied for you. I can't wait for you to move in."

By the time Eddie got out of the shower, Donna had thrown all of his worldly goods into two black garbage bags, and dumped them out on the front lawn. She told him, "Get your sorry ass out of here before I call Suzie and tell her who you really are!"

Messages from the other side: During Donna's sessions, both her mother and her father came through to apologize for telling her to stay married to her husband. Her mother came through to say, "We had no idea about all his womanizing, drinking, and all the verbal abuse he heaped on you. You never told us about that. Had we known, we'd never have told you to stay with him."

Her father came through to say, "I'm sorry. I should have known that something must have been really wrong in your marriage for you to want out of it. As for Eddie, he was a liar when we knew him, and he's an even bigger liar now. Get rid of him. He's never going to change."

Eddie's father came through as well to say, "Eddie always judged me harshly for my womanizing, addictions, and shady business deals. What we judge, we become, and Eddie is even worse than I ever was, and if you know what's good for you—get out now!"

These messages from the other side really helped Donna to come to that place of self-love and acceptance. She had a harder time forgiving herself for being duped again by the Prince Who Becomes the Beast than forgiving Eddie for all of his wrongdoings.

I told her, "If we don't learn the right lessons from the ending of one relationship, unfortunately, the next person brought to us will be more like our ex then we care to know. What you didn't learn from your ex-husband you learned from Eddie."

In a nutshell, Donna's karmic lessons were these: 1) Learn to trust your gut, and if your gut tells you someone is lying, then that's all you need to learn. 2) *The Unfixables* never change. 3) Learn when enough is enough and be loyal to those people who deserve your loyalty.

———❧———

The New Golden Rule: Trust your own inner voice.

———❧———

Ten Degrees of Manipulation

Manipulators are geniuses at catching us at moments of weakness.

Not all manipulators are created equal. If we were to place manipulation on a scale of one to ten, most people would fall somewhere in the middle range. Most people aren't smart or mean enough to be a ten, and we can be grateful for that. Hitler was certainly a ten.

The more benign manipulators are like tumors that you can cut out or leave, depending upon how they're affecting you.

Other manipulators are like malignant tumors, and cutting them out and other more invasive strategies have to be employed to make sure they don't come back to destroy you at a later time.

Just remember that if your gut tells you someone is up to no good or is lying, then that's all the proof that you need. Don't stick around until you get a knife in your back, because you still give everyone the benefit of the doubt.

Questions for Self-Analysis

1. Look over the list of the ways people manipulate others. What kind of manipulative behaviors are you guilty of?

2. Who are the people in your life who have manipulated you in the past? For instance, was your mother a manipulator? Look over the list of ways in which people manipulate us. What techniques did this person or these people use to get you to do what they wanted?

3. What kind of manipulation works best on you?

4. Who is still pushing all your guilt buttons?

5. In a romantic relationship, have you ever fallen for the Prince or Princess Who Became the Beast? In other words, did this person tell you everything that you wanted to hear, and did this person give you the impression that he or she was an entirely different person then he or she turned out to be? Has this situation happened more than once in your life?

6. List *The Unfixables* who are still in your life. Why are you keeping this person or these people in your life?

"The Turtle and the Scorpion": Ruminate on This One

Jāmī, whose full name was Mowlanā Nūr Od-dīn abd Or-rahmān Ebn Ahmad, was a fifteenth-century Persian scholar, mystic, and poet. His ancient poem, "The Turtle and the Scorpion," is an allegorical poem that sums up the theme of this chapter: the good have to watch their own backs, since evil beings will drag anyone or anything down with them. This parable is as old as time, and there are many other versions and variations on this allegory as well that you might want to research for yourself.

In a nutshell, the poem tells the tale of the happy turtle, merrily swimming down the river, minding his own business, when he encounters a scorpion that can't make it across the river on his own.

The cunning scorpion asks the turtle for a ride, and the turtle says, "You must be crazy. If I take you on my back, you're going to sting me, and then I'll drown."

The scorpion, a conniving arachnid, replies, "Hey, if you go down, I go down. So, think about it. Why in the world would I do that?"

The turtle thinks about this for a moment and then says, "You're right. There isn't any sense to you stinging me, if you'd go down with me. Hop on!"

Halfway across the river, the scorpion stings the turtle. As they both began sinking to the bottom, the turtle asks, "Why would you do this? Bring us both down? This whole thing makes no sense to me."

The scorpion, about to die, answers, "There's nothing logical about the situation at all. It's just my nature."

Ultimately, we must learn that there are some creatures on this earth that can't stop their evilness, no matter what. If, time and time again, you fall prey to these kinds of creatures, then there is no one to blame but yourself. In truth, the blame in these no-win situations must be equally shared by both the victim and the perpetrator. If **The Great Enablers** refuse to recognize and understand this truth, and go on believing that they can change others, then they will continue to be used and abused by **The Unfixables**.

––––––––––

Remember: If you carry the cross and the baggage of **The Unfixables** *on your back, then fully expect, sometime in the near or distant future, to go down like a sinking Titanic with them.*

––––––––––

The New Golden Rule: You can't change the world, but you can certainly change yourself.

––––––––––

Your Mantra from This Day Forward

People will always try to cast me in the role of victim, but it's only *my own* dysfunction that will allow me to take on that role. I choose to heal my issues so that I will never be victimized again.

Two

Your First So-Called Good Trait:
Your Need to See the Good in Everyone
Or, I See the World through Rose-Colored
Glasses

Lies can never become truth; no matter how many people believe them.

—Cindi Sansone-Braff

This chapter will teach you why "See no evil, hear no evil, speak no evil," is the root of all evil. I think Edward Burke said it best: "In order for evil to flourish, all that is required is for good men to do nothing."

If good people can't see evil in the first place, then they can't do anything to stop it. In the last chapter, you read about the different kinds of manipulators. Remember the Deniers? Good people who hide their heads in the sand and act like Pollyanna are guilty of this kind of manipulation. Not seeing evil or not seeing what's under your nose is the whole "Pink-Elephant-in-the-room-thing," where no one acknowledges the real issues, although they're so obviously staring everyone right in the face. There's a definite big payoff in living in a deep state of denial: If we pretend that something isn't happening, then we don't have to do anything to correct the situation.

When you're in a state of deep denial, you're making a subconscious choice to not address a particular situation. For instance, if you suspect that your child is using recreational drugs, but you do nothing to check up on this child, or you avoid confronting your child about the situation, then you're deliberately choosing to deny a very dangerous and life-threatening problem. We all know that once we open a can of worms, we're going to have to deal with whatever comes squirming out at us. Just know that if you deny the existence of very real problems and issues, then you become part of that problem and not part of the solution. Denying that problems exist doesn't mean that they're not there. Sooner or later, the truth comes out.

Seeing only the good in others is another form of denial. Learning to see the bad and ugly in people is the first step you must take if you want to lead a saner, happier life.

Where did this "seeing-only-the-good-in-others" mentality come from, anyway? For one thing, the dogma of most major organized religions brainwashes people to believe that good people should see only the good in others. Most of us were taught that it is godlike to forgive, to turn the other cheek, to help others, to put others first, to be loyal, and to believe that it is our job to be our brother's keeper. Good people have just learned these lessons too well. They can be too forgiving, even when people hurt them time and time again. They turn the other cheek so often that they're continually slapped silly. *The Great Enablers* help others and put others first so much that they become living martyrs. They're loyal to the point of insanity. They often continue to remain loyal to *The Unfixables* no matter how often these people have stabbed them in the back. As for being their brother's keepers, *The Great Enablers* rarely punish their family members, even if they've raped and robbed them. It's my intention in writing this book to show you how this kind of thinking has allowed *The Unfixables,* since the dawn of time, to get away with murder.

Keep Your Eyes Open and Proceed with Caution

When driving around a dangerous blind curve, you certainly don't think, "What I don't know won't hurt me." You know to keep your eyes open and proceed with caution.

This same kind of logical reasoning applies to any and all precarious situations we encounter in life. Yes, you have to keep moving forward, but to do so with blinders on never portends a happy ending. Look before you leap!

The Hitler Syndrome

The Great Enablers not only see the best in people, but they also bring out the best in people. The combination of those two traits, 1) seeing only the good in others, and 2) bringing out the best in others, is a deadly combination. Wait? Did you say, deadly? Yes, and I meant it. I call this the Hitler Syndrome. If you're one of *The Good-to-a-Fault People,* then meditate on this: if you were dining with Hitler and Mussolini in 1940, you would *not only see* the good in them, but you would also *bring out the best* in these two bastards as well. You'd be thinking how Mussolini has the trains running on time, and how Hitler was named *Time Magazine's* Man of the Year in 1938. As you broke bread with these two men, you'd think, "What perfect dining companions I have tonight." *Frightening, isn't it?* Your gut or psychic ability might even be telling you "something isn't kosher here," but many organized religions have taught that psychic abilities are the devil at work. Both the Old Testament and the New Testament have many references to the evil of psychic abilities. The Old Testament even threatened those who used psychic abilities with horrific punishment such as being put to death by stoning. For this reason, ***The Good-to-a-Fault People*** have learned to ignore their gut instincts. Call it what you will—psychic ability, our gut, or our intuition—if we trusted our own inner guidance, we would be fooled much less often by ***The Unfixables*** of the world.

Who benefits from the good people of the world not trusting their gut feelings, their intuitive powers? The Hitler-types and all the other manipulators of the world, that's who.

The day that you begin trusting your gut instincts above all else, is the day your life gets better. Then no one can pull the wool over your eyes or get you to do things that you really don't want to do.

Your so-called good traits of seeing only the good in others and bringing out the best in others, combined with your tendency to ignore your intuition, will set you up for one heartbreak after another—both personally and professionally. The solution: see what's in front of your face, trust your gut, and react accordingly.

Four Ways to Keep One Step Ahead of *The Unfixables*

First: Learn to See the Good, the Bad, and the Ugly of People

I'm not asking you to become cynical or jaded. What is being asked of you is this: get the rose-colored glasses off and see what's in front of your face. Yes, see the good in others, but also see the bad and ugly.

Second: Learn to Trust Your Gut

If your gut tells you something is rotten in Denmark, then follow the stench, until you find out where it's coming from. Good people tend to think that everyone else thinks like they do. No, they don't. Because good people are trusting, they tend to take at face value what others tell them. They rarely check up on others.

Blindly believing that others are faithful or honest may seem like the Christian thing to do, but I honestly don't believe that God wants you to practice the art of denial.

Good people tend to trust others, but many times, by doing this they have put their own children in harm's way. For example, the assumption that if you put your children in Catholic school, then they will always be surrounded by good people has proven to be a big mistake for countless numbers of people. Far too many children have been sexually abused by priests, and far too many children have not been believed when they claimed that this happened or was happening to them. Children are molested by coaches, teachers, and babysitters far too often, because the good people of the world never check up on people to find out if they have any prior arrests, disciplinary actions, or a history of mental illness. They trust that someone else has screened these people or they wouldn't be in the positions they are. My advice to all parents is this: do your own homework and your own research before you entrust your children to anyone, and if your gut tells you that this person isn't good, follow that instinct. It's far better to be safe than sorry.

If your gut tells you someone is lying, then trust that they are. What you don't know can hurt you. In this day and age, denying that someone is cheating on you can cost you your life, if that cheating person contracts a deadly venereal disease that you later catch.

Third: Learn to Watch Your Back

Just because you're bringing out the best in a particular person—say, for instance, Hitler—that doesn't mean that you're immune to landing in an oven. It's our own form of narcissism to believe that if we're good to someone, then that means they'll always be good to us. Realize that if you're dealing with a person who regularly hurts others, it won't be long before you, too, will be stabbed in the back by that very same person.

Fourth: Beware of People Who Make *You* Feel Guilty

Good people tend to be plagued with guilt, somehow believing that *it's all their fault.* Once again, let me point out that this kind of thinking, the belief that everything is your fault, is your own form of narcissism and this makes you easy prey for **The Unfixables,** who regularly and routinely push everybody's guilt buttons.

I want you to ruminate on the following question for a moment: *Have I ever intentionally set out to hurt someone?*

If your answer is a resounding no, then why should you ever feel guilty? To eliminate unearned guilt, all you have to do is start looking toward your intention. If your intention in walking away from people is not to hurt them, but self-preservation, then that is coming from a place of self-love. Know then that any guilt you feel is unearned and will be processed by the universe, and this, too, shall pass.

Learn to ask yourself in any given circumstance: *What is my intention in doing this?*

Good people have a hard time saying "no," and find themselves financially, emotionally, physically, and psychologically exhausted. After a while, you aren't mad at the people who are taking advantage of you—you're mad at yourself for allowing it. Start paying attention to how often you agree to do something that you really don't want to do. Stop being a martyr. Carry only your own cross, and come to see that saying no doesn't mean that you're a bad person.

I have an expression: *you lost me at the guilt.* When someone tries to guilt me into doing something I'd rather not do, then I see this person as a manipulator and that makes it all the easier to just say no!

Dogma is Dead

God is dead. God remains dead. And we have killed him.

—Friedrich Nietzsche

With all due respect to the great German philosopher, Friedrich Nietzsche, I like to think that God is still very much alive. I, in fact, firmly believe that *God isn't dead. Dogma is.*

Much of what you read in this book will appear to contradict what you've learned in Sunday school. I won't even get into the hotly debated topic as to whether the Bible has been tampered with or not, but I think we can all agree on the fact that every piece of writing, including all of the sacred texts that have ever been written, can and have been used, abused, and interpreted in any number of ways by people in hot pursuit of proving their own points.

It's my contention in writing this book, which inevitably will be seen by some as their "saving grace" and by others as the work of the anti-Christ, to point out that **The Self-Serving Narcissists** of the world, and there are no shortages of these on the planet, are the ones who made a lot of the rules, such as "You've made your bed; now lie in it," or "Honor me no matter what." In your heart of hearts, do you honestly believe that God would ever tell you, one of his beloved children, that you must endure pain and suffering all the days of your life, because you have fallen in love with the Prince or Princess Who Later Became the Beast?

Ironically, it's only the good people who have tried to respect these rules, while the manipulative powers that be have used them to control others, as they blatantly or quietly, break every rule themselves. This is certainly why "the good die young." So many good people would rather die than rip the blinders off and see the world as it truly is: a place where good and evil exist side by side, with no clear lines of demarcation where we can say, "Evil is over there, but not here." That kind of thinking is at best naïve and at worst deadly.

This is the kind of twisted thinking that allowed the heroin epidemic on Long Island to spread like wildfire. Suburbanites, believing that heroin is a ghetto problem, couldn't comprehend that this deadly drug was being sold in their own upscale neighborhoods, even in playgrounds, parks, and public and private schools. Far too many young people died of overdoses before parents, living in a state of deep denial, came to grips with the fact that evil was in their own backyards and not a train ride away, or somewhere far, far away—for instance, on the other side of the tracks.

The Liar's Rules

I have come to call the "honor me no matter what" dictate and the "you made your bed; now lie in it" dictate the liar's rules.

Firstly, good people don't think that they own others, nor would they ever enslave others or manipulate others to act against their own wills, under any circumstances. Secondly, when you're a good person, you don't need threats, force, or fear to keep people with you. They will stay with you out of love. Manipulative people have used the fear of God or the fear of retribution and vengeance for far too long in an effort to keep the good people in line. *The Unfixables* never go an eye for an eye. No, they go for your left eye, your right arm, and your firstborn in an effort to terrorize you and anyone else who bears witness to what they've done.

The new twenty-first-century spiritual revolution will occur when the good people stand together saying, "*We will honor those people who deserve honoring, and we will punish those people who trespass against us. For this is the way of God. The good shall inherit the earth and evil shall fall asunder.*"

One last thought. Being a good person doesn't mean that you never do anything wrong. Being a good person means that you recognize that you've done something wrong, and you learn from that mistake. Good people do what they can to rectify their mistakes and to pay for those mistakes. Good people make plenty of mistakes, because they're only human. The difference between good people and *The Unfixables* is that good people take responsibility for their behaviors and don't blame others for their wrong-doings. *The Unfixables* never take responsibility for their mistakes, because they truly believe that it wasn't their fault in the first place.

I believe that people can take what they want, but they have to pay for it. I further believe that all people have to stop expecting others to pay for their mistakes, clean up their messes, or carry their crosses.

The Truth about the Fifth Commandment

Don't think that I came to send peace on the earth. I didn't come to send peace, but a sword. For I came to set a man at odds against his father, and a daughter against her mother, and a daughter-in-law against her mother-in-law. A man's foes will be those of his own household.—Matthew 10:34–37

Do you truly believe that God would ask us to blindly obey and give allegiance to our parents: that is, to honor our father and mother no matter what? I believe that this problem was one of the main issues that Jesus was sent down on earth to address, and that the above quote clearly states this thinking: "… For I came to set a man at odds against his father, and a daughter against her mother, and a daughter-in-law against her mother-in-law. A man's foes will be those of his own household." Jesus was trying to let people know that we need not blindly obey authority or blindly honor our parents or elders, if they're not acting in a morally correct manner.

I, for one, strongly believe, that God would not ask us to honor parents who have emotionally, physically, psychologically, or sexually abused us. Nor would he ask us to honor parents who have stolen from us, be it in the form of an inheritance or in any other financial situation.

The Legacy of Sexual Abuse

Many of my clients have been victims of sexual abuse by parents, grandparents, or other family members. If a person's father has sexually abused him or her, this person will go through a lot of angst to try to understand the world, him- or herself, God, and society.

Sexual predators take advantage of children's love and trust, and then betray them. This kind of abuse can result in those children growing up with mental illness, drug and alcohol dependencies, sex addiction, rage issues, and a whole host of physical ailments as well. As a society, we have to stand together to see that all sex offenders are punished to the full extent of the law, regardless of who they are.

Sadly, few people who have been sexually abused by their parents, grandparents, or other family members have ever had them arrested. Consequently, these predators have remained a danger to other loving, trusting children. Sexual abuse of children is not only a criminal offense, but it's a crime against humanity.

Anyone who has been molested by a family member has a moral obligation to report the crime. If this crime goes unpunished, and this pedophile later goes on to hurt another child, the person who was in a position to stop the horrid act from ever taking place again is equally responsible for this deplorable action. Do not walk away in peace from sexual abuse without alerting others to the very real possibility that this kind of predatory action can and probably will take place again, unless this pedophile is held accountable for his or her actions.

My question to all of you who are reading this book is this: *Are we supposed to honor our fathers even if their horrific actions are the source of a great deal of our depression and rage issues? Are we supposed to honor mothers who allowed abuse to happen? Are we supposed to honor our mothers even if their horrific actions are the source of a great deal of our depression and rage issues? Are we supposed to honor fathers who allowed this to happen?*

Regina Calcaterra—A Real-Life Example of Two Parents Who Didn't Deserve Honoring: A Mother Who Abused Her and a Father Who Denied Her

Regina Calcaterra was the chief deputy executive of Suffolk County when Superstorm Sandy swept through the East Coast of the United States in late October 2012. After assisting Long Islanders in the recovery from Hurricane Sandy, she was appointed executive director of New York State's Moreland Commission on Utility Storm Preparation and Response by Governor Andrew Cuomo. After seeing this accomplished, smart, attractive woman in the news, many people would be shocked to read her memoir, *Etched in Sand,* published by William Morrow in 2013. It is the true story of five Long Island siblings who survived an unspeakable childhood.

I am blessed to personally know Regina, and when the galley of her soon-to-be-released memoir arrived at my home, I felt honored to have been chosen to read it before it hit the bookstores.

With great courage, Regina tells the story of her abusive childhood from the vantage point of her thirteen-year-old self. The book opens with Regina and her other siblings packed like sardines in a broken-down jalopy. With all their worldly goods stuffed into black garbage bags crowding the trunk, their chain-smoking mother, whom they refer to as Cookie, is manning the wheel. Cookie, the mother from hell, has a list of warrants out for her arrest, including one for drunk driving, and nothing Cookie does or doesn't do much surprises any of the children. Their destination is another new place to live, which they all know won't be their home for long, but at least for a while they won't be sleeping in the car or living in a homeless shelter. The list of crimes committed against these children by their mother, truly one of **The Unfixables,** includes: verbal abuse, beatings, leaving them alone for weeks and months at a time without money, food, or even heat in the winter. Meanwhile, their mother always seems to have enough money for booze, drugs, and cigarettes.

Regina, a mere child herself, is left alone to take care of her younger siblings after her older sister flies the coop. Regina has no choice but to steal food for the little ones, and when little is left over for herself, she dines on vinegar and bees to stay alive.

This frightening, Dickensian tale is nothing short of heartbreaking. It recounts how the five children were tossed from one foster home to another, enduring homelessness and substandard living conditions, all because of their mother's selfishness, addictions, narcissism, meanness, and sociopathic tendencies. The children lived in an anxiety-producing state of constant dread, since there was no harsher judge of their behaviors then their crazed mother, who doled out beatings and verbal abuse for the slightest infractions. They dreaded being alone without any parental supervision, but they feared even more their mother's drunken returns home, when she would subject then to unprovoked, rage-filled tirades. They further dreaded the thought of being separated from each other, should they once again be dumped in different foster homes and subjected to all kinds of crimes committed against them. This fear of separation was so great that the children made a pact to try and stay together no matter what, even if it meant lying about their living conditions and their mother's abuse to social services, the police, and teachers.

The level of abuse, mental, physical, psychological, emotional, and sexual, that Regina and her siblings endured makes reading this book a very painful experience. The fact that so many people in a position to help these children failed them adds salt to their wounds. A further blow to Regina's already battered self-esteem occurred when she confronted her biological father, and he turned her away, claiming that there was no way that he could have fathered her.

At the age of fourteen, Regina, already suffering from malnutrition, was beaten brutally by her mother. She was so obviously neglected and abused that she could no longer keep her vow of silence in order to keep her siblings together. Although coming clean with the abuse allowed her to become legally emancipated from her mother, her younger siblings were then forced to live in foster homes. There they were separated from Regina's protective watch and were subjected to all kinds of abuse. Later on, when they were once again returned to their abusive mother, things took a turn for the worse for the little ones.

Regina learned the full extent of her mother's viciousness when she tried to help her younger sister, Rosie, escape the sexual abuse and physical abuse she was experiencing while living on a farm in Idaho. Regina made a call to Rosie's school to tell her guidance counselor all about the multiple abuses Rosie was experiencing. Their mother covered her tracks by lying to the guidance counselor, who actually believed her litany of lies.

If you still believe that God would tell any of us to blindly obey our parents, then you really do need to read Regina's book and reevaluate who would have made up that rule: why, pedophiles, philanderers, rage-aholics, gamblers, thieves, and child beaters—that's who.

How Bad Parents Make Good Kids Feel Bad about Themselves

When children are punished for things that they've done wrong, this becomes a learning and growing experience for them. When the punishment fits the crime—no allowance, being grounded, or losing television, cell phone, or other privileges for a while—these fair disciplinary actions teach children, through behavior modification, how to behave better in the future. Children can accept that when they've done something wrong—for instance, not doing their schoolwork, stealing, or being mean to one of their siblings—some sort of punishment is in order. In these instances, children understand that they're being punished for their bad actions, and not because they're bad people.

However, when children do toe the line, follow the rules, do what is right and expected of them, and yet, their parents act mean, violent, or irrationally toward them, these children will grow up feeling that there must be something fundamentally wrong or bad about them to inspire their parent or parents to act the way that they do. Over the millennia, the blind honoring of parents has instilled in children the false belief that there are no bad parents, only bad kids.

For example, one of my clients, Sandy, first came to me for a session soon after her ninety-year-old mother died. She explained to me that she was the youngest of three children, and that she had spent most of her childhood trying her best to avoid her mother's harsh ridiculing and fast fists by doing everything that was expected of her. Sandy was polite and obedient, did well in school, and helped with the household chores without any prompting; and yet, her mother never had a kind word to say to her and found fault with everything she did. Never more than two or three days went by when Sandy didn't receive a beating. She had to wear long sleeves, even in the summer, to hide all the bruises.

On the other hand, her mother would let her two older brothers get away with murder. Her brothers would steal, cut out of school, and lie about everything, but her mother would always make excuses for them, and even laugh as she retold the tales of their latest escapades, saying, "Boys will be boys!"

Sandy's father worked long hours, and when he came home from work, he was too tired to deal with much of anything. There were times when he witnessed one of his wife's tirades, but he never did anything to stop them, and he usually just walked into another room until the beatings stopped. He died of pancreatic cancer when Sandy was sixteen, and things at home went from bad to worse.

At eighteen, Sandy married Mike, a man she didn't even like, let alone love, just to get out of the house. She stayed with him for more than two decades, even though he never had anything good to say about her, never worked for more than a few months at a time, and when he drank, which was just about every day, he was mean, violent, and abusive to her. They moved from one state to another, because her husband seemed to burn his bridges wherever they went, and after a while, she stopped unpacking their things and just lived out of boxes.

Sandy told me, "It was a blessing that we never had any children, because I know he would have abused them, too." Sandy cried herself to sleep most nights, and often wondered how much more of Mike she could take. She looked me right in the eyes when she said, "I was just shy of forty when that bastard dropped dead of a massive heart attack. That day was the happiest day of my life."

On her fiftieth birthday, Sandy got a call from one of her brothers. "Mom had a stroke," he said. "You gotta get your ass back here to take care of her."

The next day, Sandy quit her job and moved halfway across the country to take care of her mother. For five years, Sandy waited on her mother hand and foot. Throughout this time, her mother never had a kind word to say to her. She mocked Sandy about her weight gain, the way that she wore her hair, and basically tormented and tortured Sandy, right up until the day she died.

When Sandy first came to me, her mother had only passed away the month before. Sandy was guilt ridden and depressed. She thought that she hadn't been a good daughter, although she said, "God knows I tried, but it wasn't easy. There were times when I just lost it with her…" Sandy broke down at that moment. "It's all my fault—everything," she told me. "I just feel bad all the time. I've always tried to do what's right, but it just never turns out that way."

Her mother had beaten her down so much that even Sandy believed that she was a bad person and that she hadn't done enough for her mother. I told Sandy how *The Unfixables* instinctively know to treat one child badly and the rest like royalty. It's the child who parents treat like a piece of crap who will be there to wipe their butts when they die, because that child will still try—even at the hour of a parent's death—to get his or her love and approval.

I further told Sandy that she would have to learn to love herself the way she would have loved her own daughter. I asked, "If someone emotionally, physically, psychologically, and verbally abused your daughter, how angry would you be?"

Sandy said that she would be furious if those things happened to her daughter. I said, "Then anger is the right emotion for you to feel."

I then explained to her that depression is anger turned inward. "You need to write a letter to your deceased mother telling her twenty-five reasons why you have a right to be angry with her, so that you can get this anger out of your system. Do not make a saint out of your mother now that she's mercifully gone. Remember the good, the bad, and the ugly of her. Do not rewrite history!" "Next," I continued, "you need to write a letter to your father telling him why you have a right to be mad at him. Your mother was crazy, but what was your father's rationale for allowing her to abuse you all the time? Finally, you're to write a letter to your deceased husband listing a hundred reasons why he owes you an apology for all the abuse he heaped on you. Your final assignment is to write a letter to yourself, forgiving yourself for allowing others to treat you badly, and then you're to vow to yourself that you will never allow anyone to mistreat you again."

Sandy has since told me that her guilt and anger are gone, and that she has finally come to see that she was a good daughter and that she never deserved to be treated the way that she was. She had to take her brothers to court to get her rightful inheritance, and they have since disowned her, which makes her supremely happy! She now has a job she loves, and she's working on her self-esteem issues. She has even told me that she is ready to give love another shot!

Messages from the other side: During that first session, Sandy's mother came through to say she was sorry. I had to tell Sandy to take this apology with a grain of salt, since her mother was recently dead, and I felt that her mother wasn't being truly sincere. I told her that some people immediately change for the better after they die. They don't have their bodies; therefore, they don't have their addictions or other physical pain, and they're infinitely better off. But if a person was truly one of **The Unfixables,** he or she may not change even in spirit. These people may be incapable of changing even if they walked the earth again for ten more lifetimes.

Keep in mind that when I'm talking to the dead, I don't hear voices; rather, I hear them as thoughts in my own head that I intuitively know are not originating from my own mind. When Sandy's mother came through from the other side, in my head, I heard her screaming at me and threatening me. In my mind, I told her mother that she had no power over me and was in no position to harm me. I reminded her that she was in a very low realm in the afterlife, but that there were even lower ones, and if she continued her death-side tantrum, she would be locked in a realm where no one could hear her. I advised her to remain silent if she had nothing good to say. That immediately shut her up! I told Sandy that at a later date, a year or two from now, her mother might have learned enough while in spirit to truly make some amends to her.

As for Sandy's father, he came through crying. He said that he should have done more to protect her from her mother, and that he was waiting for the letter from Sandy telling the many reasons why he had failed her. Sandy started crying, when I told her that he was asking her to forgive him.

I told Sandy that her father was sincere in his apologies. Next he revealed all the times that he had guided her and protected her from the other side, including one time when she had gotten into a car accident that should have been a fatal one, and yet she walked out without a scratch. He told her that he had protected her from the grave much better than he had ever protected her on earth.

A few months later, Sandy came for another reading. She told me that her father's messages went deep inside of her and seemed to heal something. She had also written the letters to her mother, father, and dead husband.

In that session, her dead husband, Mike, came through. He told Sandy about his childhood sexual abuse that he had never processed on earth. He asked her to forgive him for all his rage. I explained to Sandy that sexually abused people have an endless amount of rage, and that toxic love serves the purpose of allowing them to vent some of this rage behind closed doors. Mike told her that he was sorry for all the bad things that he had done to her. I told her that Mike has worked very hard to heal his issues, but that still doesn't mean she has to see him in the afterlife.

Sandy said, "I gave him till death do us part, but I have no intention of ever seeing him again."

I said, "You are karmically free of him and owe him nothing. You can forgive Mike the man, but not his actions, and close the door on him."

The New Golden Rule: We're asked to sacrifice our lives for people who would do the same for us.

Questions for Self-Analysis

1. Spend the next fifteen minutes listing all the times in your life that you gave someone the benefit of the doubt, and in doing so, you wound up hurt, either emotionally, physically, psychologically, or financially. (You could fill a whole book with your answers to this question alone!)

2. Remember a recent time when your gut told you that someone wasn't who he or she professed to

be, and yet, you second-guessed your gut and went along with whatever this person wanted, only to find yourself stabbed in the back by this person.

3. List five times in the last few years when someone guilted you into doing something that you didn't really want to do.

4. Did a family member, husband, parent, sibling, child, or grandparent ever commit a crime against you, for instance by stealing an inheritance, physically hurting you, or sexually abusing you, and did you allow this person or these people to get away with that crime? Why did you feel that this kind of behavior was acceptable? If you could do it all again, would you do anything different, and why?

Three

Your Second So-Called Good Trait:
You're Loyal to a Fault
Or, I Made My Bed and Now I Lie in It

We have come to a point where it is loyalty to resist, and treason to submit.

—Carl Schurz, American statesman and reformer, and Union Army general in the American Civil War

Loyalty implies fidelity or the quality of being faithful to a person, cause, or duty. This fidelity is as compelling as any sworn vow and as binding as any signed contract. Loyalty further demands that we be steadfast in our allegiance to this person, cause, or duty, even in the face of temptation to renounce, betray, or desert these obligations. Loyalty also carries within it a sense of piety, meaning once we have given our pledge to a cause or person, we feel in our hearts it is our sacred duty to carry out this pledge, even if it means great personal sacrifice, including the loss of our own lives, if necessary.

The Four Tenets of Loyalty

1. We must always, without exception, be first and foremost loyal to God, and to righteous people, just causes, and ultimately to our own higher consciousness and conscience.

2. In the end, we must be loyal to our own core beliefs, values, and immortal selves.

3. What we haven't been taught is that loyalty is a two-way street. Good people, aka *The Great Enablers*, seem to get involved in lopsided agreements at work, play, and every which way in between, and the agreement to be good, loyal, trustworthy, and honest is only honored by the righteous, and not by *The Self-Serving Narcissists* of the world. The insane part is that this fidelity persists in *The Great Enablers* even when the person, cause, or organization in which they have believed has failed them time and time again. Once you come to understand that loyalty is earned and a two-way street, you will quickly clear your life of liars, cheaters, and backstabbers.

4. We're asked to be loyal only to those persons, causes, or organizations that are serving the highest good for all. We're not expected to be loyal to a person, cause, or an organization if that loyalty demands that we compromise our true values and beliefs.

The Real Moral Dilemma Loyalty Poses

The real question of loyalty is: To whom, how, when, where, and why should we be loyal? This is a question that all human beings have struggled with since the dawn of time.

We're taught from early on to be loyal to friends, significant others, the world at large—including our church, state, profession, and teams or organizations—and, of course, our families.

Keep in mind that first and foremost loyalty is something a person, cause, or organization has to earn and continue earning.

As we discussed in the previous chapter, most of us have been taught to be loyal to our family members no matter what. The Ten Commandments themselves have instilled this belief with the concept of Honor Thy Father and Honor Thy Mother. These commandments have tried the consciences and hearts of good people for millennia, as we already discussed in the previous chapter. Historically, parents have beaten their children and, if they so desired, molested them, and in the overwhelming majority of these cases, the offending parent was never punished for these crimes. Loyalty becomes a liability when we use it as an excuse to condone amoral and illegal activities.

To add insult to injury, family members have been brainwashed to not air their dirty laundry; to ignore the pink elephant in the room; to make saints out of the dead; to put a slab on it and never talk about what was done to them; to not rock the boat; to let sleeping dogs lie; and by all means—to never rattle the skeletons in the closet.

The brilliance of the invention of talk therapy in the late nineteenth century was that behind closed doors, you got to tell one person, who was sworn to keep your family secrets secret, the truth of what happened behind your closed doors.

The New Golden Rule: We're only expected to be loyal to people, organizations, and causes when those people, organizations, and causes act in a morally correct manner. Otherwise, all bets are off!

Daniel Ellsberg: When a Whistle-Blower is a True Patriot

Can it really be a crime to expose a crime?

—Daniel Ellsberg, the man who leaked the Pentagon Papers

I had the great pleasure of meeting Dr. Daniel Ellsberg back in August of 2010 at Guild Hall in East Hampton, after a screening of a film about his life entitled *The Most Dangerous Man in America.*

This documentary reveals how Dr. Ellsberg's early life and career helped shape the man who would later become known as one of the greatest whistle-blowers of all times. It's fascinating to watch his journey from Marine Corps platoon leader in the mid- to late 1950s to a leading peacenik in the late 1960s and early 1970s.

After receiving a PhD in Economics in 1962 from Harvard University, Dr. Ellsberg went to work in the Pentagon under Robert McNamara, and later served in Vietnam as a civilian working in the State Department, for General Edward Lansdale, before returning to work at RAND Corporation. While working at RAND in 1967, he contributed to a top-secret study, which was officially titled *United States—Vietnam Relations, 1945–1967: A Study Prepared by the Department of Defense,* written at the request of Defense Secretary Robert McNamara. The media would later dub this study the Pentagon Papers.

In 1969, Ellsberg and his colleague, Anthony Russo, spent months secretly making several sets of photocopies of this massive, forty-seven-volume, seven thousand-page document, an awesome task back in the predigital days. Ellsberg knew that these documents revealed unconstitutional actions taken by a succession of presidents. These papers proved, among other things, that the United States had escalated the Vietnam War with bombings of Cambodia and Laos and other Marine Corps attacks, and that these reports were never reported to the media. The most shocking revelation of all was that four presidents, from Truman to Johnson, had all hidden from the public their true intentions and their true actions.

The following year, Ellsberg was troubled by a conscience that wouldn't let him close his eyes to this massive cover-up. At first, he tried to go in-house with this study. He went to several politicians and political leaders, including Nixon's national security advisor, Henry Kissinger, asking that they help him in his quest to disclose these findings to the American people. Needless to say, those efforts proved fruitless.

In 1971, Ellsberg felt that it was his moral obligation to bring this information to the American public. It was then that he decided to give a copy of this document to the *New York Times* reporter Neil Sheehan. The *New York Times* staff sought legal counsel before publishing these papers. Although they were advised not to publish them, after considerable deliberations, they did so, believing that the press had a First Amendment right to publish data that would help people better understand their government policies.

The Nixon administration obtained a federal injunction to stop the papers' publication, but upon appeal, the case was lost in the Supreme Court.

Ellsberg and Russo then faced charges under the Espionage Act of 1917, and a host of other charges, including theft and conspiracy, were added on as well, carrying a maximum sentence of 115 years. Due to governmental misconduct and illegal evidence gathering, the charges were dismissed in 1973, after federal district judge William Matthew Byrne Jr. declared a mistrial.

The legacy of Dr. Ellsberg's heroic actions set in motion a chain of events that ended not only the Nixon administration, but ultimately the Vietnam War.

The leaking of the Pentagon Papers, one of the greatest whistle-blowing sagas of all times, is an example of a man being loyal to his own conscience, God, and humanity above all else—no matter what the personal consequences.

To learn more about this whistle-blowing patriot, read *Secrets: A Memoir of Vietnam and the Pentagon Papers,* which is Dr. Ellsberg's autobiographical account of how he went from a gung-ho advisor to the State and Defense Departments to impassioned antiwar crusader.

The Liars Tell Half-Truths

The Self-Serving Narcissists of the world are famous for shouting slogans that are filled with half-truths.

We've all heard the expression, "My country, right or wrong," and we usually hear it in reference to something that our government is doing that it shouldn't be doing. Yet we, as American citizens, are expected to back our government and governmental authorities, even when their actions violate human rights or hurt, maim, or even kill innocent civilians.

You might be surprised to learn the that the expression "My country, right or wrong," is only the first part of a sentence attributed to Carl Schurz, an American statesman and Union Army general in the American Civil War. The whole quote is: "My country, right or wrong; if right, to be kept right; and if wrong, to be set right," which Schurz said in his remarks to the Senate, February 29, 1872.

The message is profoundly different when you put the first part of the sentence in context with the second part of the sentence. The true quotation does not imply blind obedience to our government; rather, it implies that each of us has a moral obligation to fix what might be wrong with our country.

The above example of a quotation that has been taken out of context and used to silence and placate the American people is perfectly illustrates how *The Self-Serving Narcissists* of the world use half-truths to manipulate others.

Is it possible that Honor Thy Father is only the first part of a statement? Could the true words of God been more like this: "Honor Thy Father, right or wrong; if right, to be kept right; and if wrong, to be set right?"

———— ✐ ————

The New Golden Rule: We can no longer live by the doctrine "My Country, Right or Wrong." Twenty-first century higher consciousness demands we reformulate our thinking, and profess, "My country—right the wrongs!"

———— ✐ ————

Remember: Telling the truth about a government that is acting amoral or committing crimes isn't an act of treason, but an act of higher consciousness. Therefore, to speak up against injustice is to be a hero who walks with an army of angels.

———— ✐ ————

A Few Historic Examples of Misplaced Loyalty

We could fill an entire book with other examples, and feel free to make a list of your own!

1. People remaining loyal to the Nazi government in the midst of massive crimes against humanity. *The Good-to-a-Fault People,* who tend to see the world through rose-colored glasses, couldn't see the evil being done, and *The Self-Serving Narcissists* and *The Unfixables* profited from the suffering and sorrow of others.

2. The Roman Catholic Church's long-term, massive cover-up of sexual abuse of children.

3. The Iran-Contra affair, which took place during the Reagan administration.

4. The My Lai Massacre: the mass murder of unarmed civilians, including women and children, in South Vietnam on March 16, 1968, committed by twenty-six US soldiers, and yet only Second Lieutenant William Calley, a platoon leader in Charlie Company, was ever convicted.

Today's Lesson in Misplaced Loyalty

Please choose any one of the above four examples of amoral and criminal activity that was covered up and do some research about that topic online or by reading articles or books on the topic to help you better understand the nature of deception and manipulation all committed in the name of misplaced loyalty.

Being Loyal to God and Humankind above All Else

These kinds of massive cover-ups and instances of misplaced loyalty to people who are doing unspeakable things have been going on since time immemorial, and will continue until we as a human species follow the dictates of higher consciousness. Higher consciousness thinking knows that: *there is nothing above, save God, and nothing below, save humankind.*

Cover-ups don't necessarily require any kind of active manipulation of facts or circumstances. The most common form of cover-up involves no action taken at all. These kinds of cover-ups are usually done in the name of loyalty to a person, cause, or organization, and follow the thinking "What they don't know can't hurt them."

Of course, nothing could be further from the truth, and nothing good ever comes out of practicing deep denial and sweeping things under the carpet. The people who are in denial believe that the benefits of covering up the act far outweigh the risk and harm that will surely come to them if the truth is made known. Later on, however, if and when the truth is revealed, the cover-up in itself becomes a bigger crime than whatever it was that these people were trying to conceal in the first place. Think about Richard Nixon and Watergate. The burglary itself pales in comparison to the efforts taken to conceal it, such as payoffs, bribes, obstruction of justice, and other crimes committed that ultimately destroyed many people's careers and lives.

How *The Self-Serving Narcissists* Cover Their Tracks

1. They deny, deny, and deny again. They try to make us think that we're crazy and nothing ever happened.
2. They lie, lie, lie, and lie some more. They just twist and turn the truth so much that we don't know which way is up.
3. They blame, shame, and scapegoat others, and in so doing, they take the heat off of themselves.
4. They bribe or convince others to help them cover up their wrongdoings, claiming it wasn't their fault in the first place, and the whole thing is just a big misunderstanding.
5. They minimize what was done: They try to convince us that it was no big deal.
6. They act as if they don't remember what happened or as if they somehow forgot the details.

7. They use intimidation tactics to scare us off or to shut us up. They attack us and our characters and claim that we have ulterior motives for destroying them.

8. They threaten to hurt us or destroy us, either personally or professionally, if we don't back off. They also threaten to hurt those we love.

9. They destroy or alter evidence, such as by deleting e-mails and text messages. They plant evidence against others, such as by tampering with our e-mails, placing something on our desks, or putting something in our possession that makes us look guilty.

10. They hire the best lawyers money can buy, so they can further manipulate the truth; this time with expert help and paid witnesses, and by stalling legal proceedings.

Questions for Self-Analysis

The main "so-called" good trait that causes many of us a great deal of grief and heartbreak is our sense of loyalty to people who don't deserve it. Are you beginning to see how crazy it is that good people think that they have to be loyal to friends or family members, even when these people have robbed from them, cheated on them, bad-mouthed them, and ruined their lives?

Answer the following eight questions to see if you're guilty of being loyal to a fault.

1. Have you ever kept someone in your life even though you know that this person has stolen from you, sexually abused you, or bad-mouthed you?

2. Have you ever kept someone working for you who wasn't doing his or her job, or who was caught

stealing from you, taking clients, or acting in a self-serving way that cost you money?

3. Have you stayed in a romantic relationship with someone who has continually cheated on you?

4. Have you kept a family member or friend in your life who is a drug addict, gambler, alcoholic, or spend-aholic, even when that person has continually reneged on promises to get help? Are you still allowing this person to hurt you emotionally, physically, psychologically, or financially?

5. Have you ever continued to loan a family member or friend money, even though that person still owes you money from past loans?

6. Have you kept these *Self-Serving Narcissists* in your life because you felt guilty to do otherwise?

7. Have you stayed in a job even after the raise, promotion, or health-care benefits you were promised never came through?

If you answered "yes" to any of these questions, you need to learn why your over-the-top loyalty is making your life hell. This book will help you see the light! Keep Reading!

———ↁↁↁ———

Remember: Grown-ups can't be victims, only volunteers. If you continue to be loyal to a fault to people who don't deserve your loyalty, you can only be angry at yourself for allowing yourself to be victimized time and time again.

As long as you go on blaming others, then you don't have to take responsibility for your own actions. You will get no sympathy from me for your self-inflicted wounds!

Stop complaining and start changing.

——⟨∞⟩——

The New Golden Rule: Until you give up victim consciousness, nothing in your life will ever change.

Four

Your Third So-Called Good Trait:
Your Belief That You Are Your Brother's Keeper
Or, It's My Job to Clean Up Your Mess and to Fix Everything and Everyone

The Great Enablers rarely ask for help, because, by nature, they're the helpers of the world. They will go to work sick, do everything that is expected of them, no matter what. They don't feign illness or claim that the dog ate their homework, because they do what they're supposed to do, even under the worst of circumstances.

Keep in mind that one of our karmic lessons in life is to learn how, when, and if to ask others for help. If you habitually *never* allow others to help you, you will eventually be given a life experience such as an illness or some sort of natural or unnatural disaster that gives you no other choice than to ask others for help. If you tend to really squirm and feel uncomfortable with asking for help, try doing it anyway. Ask someone to help you do something, fix something, or drive you somewhere. It doesn't have to be a big deal thing. Better we learn karmic lessons in small, painless ways, then in big whammy, ouch ways! Just as you feel good when you help others, you need to allow others to do the same for you, or you're depriving them of receiving that same altruistic feeling.

The Great Enablers tend to help others above and beyond the call of duty. There's a fine line between helping people and enabling them. Everyone is entitled to one rehab; one get-out-of-jail-free card, and one time their life is a sinking Titanic. After that—three strikes and they're out. *The Great Enablers* help their friends and family members way more than they should, sometimes even to the point of physical, emotional, psychological, and financial bankruptcy. In life, sometimes we just have to leave people where they fall.

Of course, good people always feel "bad" when they can't help others. This feeling "bad" then motivates good people to try and try again. *The Unfixables* of the world know this, and are adept at pushing other people's guilt buttons.

Remember: If you keep writing checks and bailing out the same people time and time again, then you're not helping them—you're enabling them.

Knowing When You're Helping and When You're Enabling

The Unfixables of the world exhibit an extraordinary sense of entitlement. This unmerited and unrealistic expectation of favorable treatment from others is ingrained in these people and makes them highly unpleasant to deal with under any circumstances.

The Unfixables will always blame others for their own shortcomings and inappropriate actions and reactions. For example, a husband punches his wife in her face and says,

"You made me do that to you, because *you* didn't listen to me." If she then calls the police (which *The Great Enablers* rarely do, as you will see in the next chapter, since they have an inability to punish the inner circle), he will then ask, "How could you put me in jail?" This man has no concept that it was his own actions that got him arrested.

Enabling is a term that's used in twelve-step recovery programs to describe the actions and behaviors that family members, lovers, and friends do in an effort to rescue those with addictions. In reality, this well-intentioned rescuing only worsens the problem by not allowing addicts to suffer the consequences of their behavior. I'm a firm believer in "the-take-what-you-want, but-be-willing-to-pay-for-it" philosophy of life. My feelings are that if you want to be a drug addict, then you take the drugs, but you pay for them: with your life, your freedom, and the loss of those nearest and dearest to you, who—God willing—one day will get fed up with enabling you. After that, you pay the monetary cost for your rehab, bail, and any other financial sinkholes that this kind of behavior inevitably brings with it. I have no intention of paying for your addiction, nor am I paying to clean up the mess you've made.

Al-Anon is an international fellowship of people, who come together to help families and friends of alcoholics. This incredible organization has a slogan, "the 3Cs," that we can all adopt in every aspect of our lives: "I didn't cause it. I can't control it. I can't cure it." When we are dealing with addicts, we need to turn the situation over to a higher power, and learn to "Let Go and Let God."

———

Remember: Bad things happen to good people when they don't get out of God's way. If you don't want negative wake-up calls of your own, stop enabling everyone, and once in a while—do allow someone to help you!

———

The New Golden Rule: People can take what they want, but they have to pay for it!

⸺ ◦∞◦ ⸺

Whatever mess anyone you know and care for has gotten him- or herself into, you need to step back and think carefully before bailing this person out. Ask yourself the following questions: Is this the first time this kind of thing has occurred? Does he or she seem genuinely remorseful? Does the person understand that what he or she has done is wrong? Should I practice tough love this time or be more compassionate and understanding?

There are no hard and fast rules here to follow, but if someone is pushing your guilt buttons and making *you feel bad* about what *he or she has done,* then that is a highly reliable indicator that this person is not remorseful, just manipulative.

Good people are plagued with unearned guilt, whereas the manipulators tend to feel no guilt at all. I have an expression, "You lost me at the guilt." I've never intentionally hurt anyone in my life; therefore, if people start guilting me into helping them, more often than not, I walk away.

If someone you love is presently practicing his or her distraction of choice—gambling, drinking, drugging, sexing, overeating, overspending, or all of the above—then rescuing this person, at this time, is an act of enabling. State that you love this person, but that you won't condone this behavior any longer. Then walk away and leave this person where he or she may fall, knowing in your heart of hearts that this is the best course of action. Of course, praying that this person doesn't fall too hard is a good thing to do as well.

If, however, this person's actions are putting others in danger, then appropriate steps must be taken to stop him or her. For instance, if this person is trying to drive under the influence, then keys must be taken or the police must be called to stop this person from endangering other innocent people.

Remember, God helps those who help themselves.

Ten Telltale Signs that You're One of *"The Great Enablers"*

1. Do you tend to help people financially, without even knowing what they might really be using the money for?

2. Do you make a lot of excuses for abuse? For example, you say things, such as: "It was the alcohol talking," or "She was beaten as a child and that's why she rages like that."

3. Do you help others cover up their mistakes?

4. Do you do other people's chores, assignments, or work, even though these people are perfectly capable of taking care of their own responsibilities?

5. Do you worry about others so much, that you barely have time to think about yourself?

6. Are you overprotective of people, feeling that it's your job to keep everybody safe?

7. Do you feel a need to rescue others?

8. Do you continue to help people simply because you feel "bad" or guilty when you try to walk away?

9. Do you feel that others can't or won't survive without you?

10. Do you think it's your job to fix everything?

11. Do you often say "yes" to people, even though you really want to say "no?"

12. Do you want everyone to like you and feel bad when they don't?

---ooo---

Remember: The world turned before you came onto this planet, and the world will go on spinning long after you leave it. The harsh truth is that The Good-to-a-Fault People have their own form of narcissism, and this is their need to be liked and their own need to feel needed.

---ooo---

Every time you enable someone, you're keeping this person from suffering the consequences of his or her own actions. You're interfering with the universe's way of teaching people. The law of karma states that every action has a reaction. You must allow people to reap what they've sown.

Why Enabling Can be Self-Serving

1. Your own fears of abandonment keep you chained to toxic and unhealthy people. You know that they'll never abandon you because they'll always need you, and you can't bear to be alone.
2. Your need to have everyone like you, and people won't like you if you leave them where they fall to wallow in their own crap.
3. It satisfies your own need to prove that you can fix people.
4. It fits with your belief that it's what God would want you to do.
5. If you have your own unresolved anger issues, staying involved with one of *The Unfixables* gives you an excuse to rage behind closed doors with this person,

and then you can go out into the world and react in a normal fashion with others.

6. It makes you feel good about yourself to help others, and you're plagued with guilt and feel "bad" if you don't help them.

7. You have a fear of rejection and a strong desire to be loved, and so you do what others ask you, no matter what the cost.

8. It satisfies your need to make peace at any price and to avoid conflict at any cost. You feel it's just easier to clean up other people's messes than to listen to their temper tantrums.

9. People always say what a saint you are and how you're always there for everyone. This makes you feel valued and important.

Give Up the Notion That It's Your Job to Fix People

First of all, recognize that your need to be needed is the reason you attract needy people into your life in the first place.

Secondly, recognize that feeling "as if everything is your fault" is a form of narcissism.

Thirdly, recognize that the need to fix others is a form of codependent behavior.

This need to fix others extends to all kinds of relationships. Fixing equates to the rescuer role in the dysfunctional triangle of behavior that we discussed in chapter 1. Admittedly, playing the rescuer is the nicer part of that triangle, and it can momentarily leave you feeling good about yourself, but it's only a matter of time before your rescuing leaves you feeling victimized and persecuted, when the rescued party turns the tables on you!

Payoffs in Being the "Fixer"

1. Needy people will never abandon you, and if you have unhealed abandonment issues, then you'll gravitate to the kind of people who can't stand on their own two feet and who will always need your undying help and assistance.

2. You're a control freak and your enabling allows you to play God and to control the outcome of any given situation.

3. Being a "Fixer" is a power position, and this gives you a feeling of self-worth and importance.

4. You like being needed by others.

5. "Fixing" appears to be unselfish and makes you appear to be a living saint. When others praise you for your unselfish acts, this makes you feel good about yourself.

6. "Fixers" cover up and clean up other people's messes to avoid the fight or ruckus that will ensue should another person find out what happened. For example, a mother secretly pays to have her son's car fixed after he cracks it up to avoid hearing her husband's tirade about her son's irresponsibility.

7. Helping others makes you feel worthy of love.

Remember: Fixing is about control—your being in control of every situation.

A Mother Learns to Stop Carrying Her Son's Cross

Five years ago, Carrie, a fifty-year-old wife and mother of three, came to me for a session. As she put it, "Everything I once believed has proven wrong." She told me that she was a grade school teacher who had always prided herself on her well-behaved young children. Up until now, she had honestly believed that good parents raised good kids. Throughout her more than a quarter of a century teaching, she had harshly judged the parents of problem children for creating those little monsters by their bad parenting skills. "I could kick myself in the ass for that one."

When I heard her say that, I had to laugh. "Carrie, God tests us on our judgments of others. I was a children's entertainer for as long as you've been a teacher, and over time I learned that some very good parents have bad kids, and some very bad parents have good kids. Children come with their own karma into this life. All of us can see this in our own families. Some children are good from day one, and they help us to be great parents. Other children are much more difficult and continually test us, and to our great dismay we become short-tempered, impatient, and find ourselves becoming the kind of parents we never wanted to be."

Carrie started crying. Her two older children were both honor students who were away at Ivy League colleges. Her youngest child, Steven, was an eighteen-year-old heroin addict, and had been one for more than four years. Carrie was at her wit's end. Steven had been in and out of rehab for years, and he was bankrupting the family with his drug habit. Besides burning through the thousands and thousands of dollars that they had spent on three different bouts of rehab for him, Steven had totaled two cars, been hospitalized with overdoses three times, and been bailed out of jail for driving under the influence twice. On top of all that, he had robbed them blind of cash and jewelry.

Carrie's husband had recently suffered a heart attack after finding out that Steven was using again. Even though Steven swore he was clean, the truth became apparent when drug dealers came banging on their front door looking for money.

"And just yesterday, he got arrested for possession of a controlled substance. I just don't know what else to do for him."

"Everyone is entitled to one rehab; one get-out-of-jail-free card; one time his or her life is a sinking Titanic, and then it's three strikes, you're out!" I said. "After that, God would ask you to get out of his way, and leave Steven where he falls, so that God and the universe can help him."

"You sound like my husband. He doesn't want me to bail Steven out of jail this time," Carrie said.

"How do you feel about that?"

"He's my son. How can I do that? I told my husband that we're Catholics. Jesus would want us to help our son."

"First of all, Carrie, God helps those who help themselves. Secondly, the symbolism of Jesus on the cross is that he's the only martyr. You need to put your son's cross down and let him carry his own cross and clean up his own mess."

"But I'm his mother."

"When Jesus was ordered to carry his cross to his crucifixion, did you hear him screaming out to his mother, 'Hey, Mary, I'm in trouble! Come carry my cross.'"

Carrie laughed, "Of, course not!"

"Then you need to stop being one of *The Great Enablers* and start telling your son to take what he wants, but pay for it. You stand by your husband, and read your son the riot act. His drug use is not only putting you and your husband in the poorhouse, but he's putting you in danger because of the drug dealers he is associating with. Tell him that you'll always love him, but you can't enable him anymore. Leave him where he fell this time—in jail. This is Steven's wake-up call. If you bail him out now, his next wake-up call might be—death. Yes, death is a wake-up call, for both the living and the dead. Pray that Steven sees the light while he's in jail."

Carrie decided to do as her husband wished, and this time, they didn't bail him out or pay for a lawyer. Steven was given a court appointed lawyer, and he was sentenced to serve one year in prison. During this time, Steven refused to talk to his mother or answer her letters. He told his cousin to tell his parents, "Thanks to the two of you, I'm rotting in jail."

After Steven was sentenced, Carrie came to me for another session and said, "I've fallen into such a deep depression, I don't think I'll ever come out of it."

I told her, "Depression is anger turned inward and a sense of hopelessness. There's nothing hopeless about your son being in jail. Some addicts change for the better because of jail. They have time to get off the drugs, and then they take a good, long look at themselves. Practice the Law of Attraction and see Steven being one of these kinds of people. As for your anger issues, who are you angry at?"

Carrie started screaming, "At everyone. I'm mad at myself for not being able to help Steven. I'm mad at my husband for giving up on our son. I'm mad at Steven for putting us through all this."

"Good, Carrie, get the anger out. We live in a drug-infested culture, and you're not alone in your agony. Perhaps you can organize a support group for other parents going through what you're going through."

And, I am proud to say, that is exactly what Carrie went on to do. She organized a support group and had experts in the field of addiction come and give lectures. She learned all she could about addiction, and this gave her a sense of hope that helped lift her depression.

The good news for Carrie and for her family is that when Steven got out of prison, he decided to turn his life around. He learned a lot about himself while locked behind bars. He realized that he'd always felt stupid compared to everyone else in his family. He was never very good in school because he didn't like it. He'd never wanted to go to college, and in his family, that made him the black sheep. He spent a great deal of his time in prison trying to figure out what he wanted to do when he grew up. One of his friends from high school began writing to him and told him that he had started a landscaping business, and if he wanted to, Steven was more than welcome to come work for him in the future. When Steven got out of jail, he decided to take his friend up on his offer, and to his surprise, he learned that he loved working outdoors. He discovered he had a real eye for landscape design, and he and his friend have made a very successful business for themselves.

Carrie recently told me that Steven thanked her and her husband for standing strong and practicing "tough love" on him. He likes to attend his mother's support group when he can, but he never misses his Narcotics Anonymous meetings.

She told me, "We take things one day at a time, and so far, so good!"

Messages from the other side: During the first session with Carrie, her deceased mother, Rose, came through. She had died a few years earlier, and she told Carrie that it was her job to watch over Steven, and that she promised to do all she could to help him. She said that she would watch over him in prison and try to pop positive and healing thoughts in his head. I told Carrie that the dead are capable of putting thoughts in our heads. Most of the time, we believe these thoughts to be our own.

After Steven got out of prison, he told his mother that he often dreamed of his grandmother, Rose. He told Carrie that in one of the dreams, Rose was standing in a huge rose garden. She called to him to join her, and she asked, "Steven, how does your garden grow?" Steven said that he told her, "Not so good." Then his grandmother hugged him and said, "In the future, you will be surrounded by flowers." Steven said the next day the letter came from his friend, the landscaper.

In a later session, Steven's friend, Brian, who had just died the month before of an overdose, came through to tell Carrie, "I'm sorry for hurting so many people. My mother doesn't deserve to be going through what she's going through. She was a good mother. I promise to help Steven. My death seems to have opened his eyes to the bad path we were on, and he realizes that he could have been me. I will guide him and try to show him that drugs aren't the answer, and I will help him to see what a good family and future he can have if he stays clean."

I believe that Brian and Grandma Rose continue to help Steven each and every day of his life.

Your Mantra

I'm not responsible for making life perfect for everyone. It's not my job to clean up everyone's messes or to carry everyone's crosses. It's not my responsibility to fix everything and everyone. It's my job to fix myself.

Janet: When Being Your Brother's Keeper Proves Deadly

Janet was raised in a very strict Italian Catholic home. The men of the family, her father, John, and her brother, Johnny Boy, were the kings of the *castello.*

Janet's father was a strict man, a rage-aholic, and irrational to boot. When she spoke to me of him, she referred to him as *il Duce.* He worked in his family's cement business and rabidly hated the work itself as well as his entire extended clan. He would often come home from work mad as hell and ready to displace this anger on his wife and children.

Janet never knew what might set her father off, and so she learned to tiptoe around him. Nonetheless, she got her share of beatings, as did her brother and her mother, and on a particularly bad night, the dog got a good beating as well.

It wasn't unusual for Janet to step in when her father was beating her mother. Janet's rationale was that her father was crazy, and he just needed to beat up someone. She felt that if she got in the middle of things, her father would forget all about her mother and just start beating on her. Janet figured that it was better if her father killed her than her mother. Her thinking was this: if her father beat her mother to death, she and her brother would be left without a mother and without a father as well, since their father would wind up in jail. She felt that if her father killed her and then went to jail for it, her brother would still have his mother to take care of him.

Even though Johnny Boy was ten years older than she was, and even though he tormented, teased, and slapped her around on an everyday basis, she still felt that she was her brother's keeper. After all, that was what she was taught in Sunday school, and that's what her mother had instilled in her since the day she was born.

Janet's mother was a miserably unhappy woman, and no matter how hard Janet tried, she could never make her mother happy. Her mother never complimented, thanked, or praised her, but that didn't stop Janet from trying to win her mother's affection and approval, all the same. Janet would clean the house, run errands for her mother, rub her back, and wait on her hand and foot. Still, her mother never acknowledged anything that Janet ever did. She would, however, notice when things weren't done, and would scream at Janet for hours at a time and ground her for weeks on end.

When Janet was seven, her father died of a massive heart attack. Janet was more relieved than sorrowful, and prayed that God would forgive her for not being sad about her own father's death. Janet thought that things in her household would actually be happier without her father. Janet was dead wrong on that one.

With her father's income gone, Janet's brother had to quit school and take his father's place in the family business. Overnight, her brother turned into her father—only worse. Johnny Boy drank almost every night after work, and he was a nasty drunk, to say the least. Stinking like booze, he would come home and spend hours at a time bullying Janet and beating her. Her mother never came to her defense, and Janet actually came to realize that her mother seemed to get some sort of sadistic pleasure out of her brother's torture of her. She came to refer to him as *il Duce Due*.

By the time Janet was seventeen, she had had enough of her brother's beatings and bullying and got a job in a local fast food establishment so that she wouldn't have to come home until late at night, when her brother was already asleep.

While working slinging hamburgers, she met Tony, the manager of the place, and two years later, they eloped. Her husband, Tony, was a kind, hardworking man who adored her. Within the first five years of marriage, Janet had three sons of her own. Janet told me, "Those years were the happiest days of my life."

Janet was thirty-five when she learned that her mother had terminal cancer. Johnny Boy had never married and still lived with their mother in the same house that they'd grown up in. Johnny Boy had been engaged once, but his fiancée had broken off the engagement after he had punched her in the face, breaking her two front teeth. From that moment on, her brother's life seemed to spiral downward. He was in and out of mental hospitals and jails, and hadn't worked in over ten years. Her mother was always making excuses for his abuse, and continued to bail him out of whatever mess he got himself into.

On her deathbed, Janet's mother made Janet promise that she would take care of her brother, no matter what. Janet, always the dutiful daughter, told her, "I will always make sure that Johnny Boy is taken care of."

Janet tried to live up to this promise, no matter how bad her brother got. *Il Duce Due* argued with her over the estate, about the way she was raising her sons, and even about the way she decorated her house. Janet tried to placate him and make him happy, even though her husband begged her to stay away from that bastard. He said, "The guy's a loose cannon, and I don't trust him."

Janet told me that she would never, as long as she lived, forget the cold, rainy November day, on the first anniversary of her mother's death, when her brother, uninvited, stopped over at her house. Her husband had just left for work, and two of her boys had just gotten on the school bus. Her youngest son was home with the flu.

The second she set eyes on Johnny Boy, she knew he was drunk, and her gut told her to leave him standing out in the rain. Still, Janet let him inside. She said, "It's eight o'clock in the morning, for God's sake, and it's pouring out. You could have killed somebody driving around like that…and, on this day of all days. Is this the way you're paying respect to our mother, by getting plastered?"

Janet doesn't remember too much of what happened after that. The details of what occurred that morning were told to the police by her eleven-year-old son, who came running into the kitchen when he heard his mother's frantic screams for help.

It seems that Janet's brother began yelling and cursing at her. He grabbed a hot cast-iron frying pan off the stovetop and began beating Janet within an inch of her life. He then grabbed a kitchen knife and stabbed her repeatedly in her legs. Her son ran out of the house to ask their next-door neighbor, who was an off-duty police officer, for help. The neighbor was able to subdue Johnny Boy, but Janet was already unconscious and lying in a pool of blood.

Janet spent five months in the hospital. She still walks with a limp, is deaf in one ear, and has a host of other health problems as a result of her brother's senseless beating.

Even after this brutal beating, it was hard for Janet to testify against her brother. She didn't want him to go to jail. She had hoped they would put him into a psych ward for treatment. She was plagued with guilt, wondering if she'd done something to provoke him. She felt that she had not lived up to her deathbed promise to her mother. Her brainwashing that she was her brother's keeper was so strong that she could barely eat or sleep for a year after her brother was sent to jail. She was extremely depressed and not in touch with the anger she felt toward her brother and toward her mother for putting her in this position.

I asked her, "If someone had done that exact thing to one of your sons, would you be angry?"

She said, "I'd be furious."

"Would you want this person to be punished to the full extent of the law?" I asked.

"Of course!" Janet answered.

"Then you need to come to that place of self-love and love yourself the way you love your sons. You have a right to be angry. You can forgive your brother, but not his actions. His actions are unforgivable. Your guilt is unearned. Your intention in putting your brother behind bars was not to hurt him, but to stop him from hurting anyone else. He could have killed one of your sons or your husband. You also have a right to be angry at your mother. She was wrong in asking you to take care of your brother, when she knew what he was capable of. Would you ever have asked one of your beloved sons to be put in such harm's way?"

In that moment, Janet's blinders fully came off. She saw that it had never been her place to carry her brother's cross or to clean up his mess. She was filled with rage at what he had done to her. She then came to see the emotional scars and the trauma that her young son now carries from witnessing the incident, and Janet was furious to think that her brother had caused her youngest so much pain. She then began to get in touch with all the pain and suffering that her hospitalization and long recovery have had on her husband and all of her sons, and she realized that her brother belonged in jail where he couldn't hurt her, her family, or anyone else for that matter.

Janet was through with being one of *The Great Enablers*. She had learned to be loyal to those who deserve her loyalty and to punish and then walk away from those who don't.

Messages from the other side: During the first session, Janet's mother-in-law, Jenny, came through loud and clear. She had passed away five years ago and loved Janet as if she were her own daughter. She thanked Janet for taking such good care of her the last year of her life, and she said, "I am so sorry about what has happened to you. When you were in the hospital, I sat with you every day, just as you had sat with me when I was dying. You have never intentionally hurt anyone in your entire life, and your intention in putting your brother in jail is to punish him for his actions and to ensure that he never hurts anyone again."

Janet's father also came through that day to ask her to forgive him. He told her that her brother was not her responsibility, and that he would watch over him while he was in jail.

It was toward one of the last sessions that her mother came through. Her mother seemed to be sincerely sorry for all she had done to Janet. She told Janet, "You were always a very good daughter, but I was never a good mother. I should never have asked you to watch over your brother. Forgive me."

Janet has told me that the messages from the other side have helped her heal inside and out. She also claims that her own psychic abilities have gotten stronger and that she gets messages from her mother-in-law almost every day.

A Sucker Is Born Every Minute

The Unfixables' mantra is this: "It isn't my fault." These people have a million excuses as to why they're in the boat they're in. These are the kinds of people who claim that because of the bad economy, they can't find work—for years and years on end. News flash: The one thing that there's no shortage of on this planet is work. People who want to work, work. *The Good-to-a-Fault People* are not above cleaning toilets, flipping hamburgers, or doing any job whatsoever, and they do whatever they're hired to do with maximum effort and to the best of their abilities.

The Unfixables love playing the victim card, claiming that they can't find work because they're too old, too young, too short, too fat, not the right gender, overqualified or under-qualified, or any one of countless reasons that we're all sup-posed to listen to and respond to with "Gee, that's too bad."

Hardworking people find work in good economies and bad economies; in fact, work finds them. Stop believing everything people say. *The Good-to-a-Fault People*, aka *The Donkey People,* do the work of eight people, day in and day out no matter what the jobless rate indicates. Think about it—How hard have you worked in your life in good economic times and in bad ones? How long were you ever out of work when you truly wanted to work? How many jobs have you done that you really didn't want to do, but you did them to put food on your family's table and to pay your debts?

Why Bad Things Happen to Good People

Have you ever wondered why bad things happen to good people? Bad things happen to good people when they won't get out of God's way. Then God has no choice but to nuke *The Good-to-a-Fault People's* world by taking their jobs, health, or homes right out from under them, so that they become too physically, emotionally, psychologically, or financially drained to help anyone other than themselves.

The Great Enablers have to learn when enough is enough. From now on, before you step up to help someone, be sure that this is your cross to carry. If you keep on carrying everyone else's crosses, God may just have to pile a few more crosses of your own on your back so that you aren't able to get in there and try to fix everything.

Learn to say to those people who are continually asking you for money, whether they are your grown children, your siblings, or any friends or family members, "Sorry, but I have no money," and then in your mind, say, "for you." Never forget that God helps those who help themselves.

The Dog Ate My Homework

Below is a list of some of the more common excuses and behaviors *The Unfixables* use to manipulate others. They always try to make others believe that all the bad things that happen to them really aren't their fault.

1. It's a bad economy, and I can't find work.
2. I had a bad childhood; therefore, I can't help myself.
3. Blame it on my astrological sign.
4. The planets are out of alignment today.
5. My therapist told me not to do it.
6. It's in my genes to act this way.
7. Nobody understands me.
8. I'm my own worst enemy.
9. This time I really believed it was going to be different
10. I could always kill myself.
11. It's all your fault!

Outsmarting *The Unfixables*

When you're dealing with *The Unfixables*, there always seems to be a lot of drama and trauma surrounding every situation. The sky always seems to be falling, and there's always a problem, catastrophe, or conflict brewing. Of course, none of this mess is their fault or their doing.

When dealing with these people, you'll have to learn to take it down a notch, make no excuses for abuse, and let go of your need to please. Learn to say, "You lost me at the guilt." I cannot say this enough—*The Great Enablers* tend to be plagued with unearned guilt, erroneously believing that everything is all their fault. This is their own form of narcissism.

Just remember: if you have never *intentionally* hurt anyone in your life, then you must come to recognize that manipulators use guilt to get their way. Eventually you will build a tougher shell that will protect you from the onslaught of guilting, shaming, blaming, and name-calling that *The Unfixables* throw your way in an effort to intimidate you into seeing things their way.

Stand firm and refuse to accept their excuses. Don't buy into their rationalizations, explanations, and lies, no matter how convincing they make their tall tales sound. These kinds of people will never admit that they did anything wrong, so the more they talk, the more they will confuse you, wear you down, and twist and turn things, so that after a while you won't know which way is up. When you're at that moment of weakness, they've got you just where they want you, confused and dazed and willing to do just about anything they ask, since you have no idea what just went down. *The Unfixables* count on others giving them the benefit of the doubt.

You have to become really attuned to the ways and means in which *The Unfixables* manipulate others. Lying is their first line of defense. They're pathological liars. *The Great Enablers* tend to think that everyone is like them; therefore, everyone tells the truth. It takes them a while to catch on to the reality that these people lie, and they lie a lot. *The Unfixables* are also guilty of lying by omission, which means they leave out important information and facts.

If lying doesn't work, they'll go on to their second line of defense—denying. They have mastered the art of denial and simply deny any wrongdoing. They'll never admit that they've done anything wrong, even when the facts are staring them and you right in the face.

They're also great at rationalizing away their behaviors by saying things such as "Everybody does this" and "Nobody cares." They're great at trivializing or minimizing the effects of their actions, and accuse others of nagging, exaggerating, and overreacting.

They're also good at using diversionary tactics. If you confront one of *The Unfixables* with a text that shows that he or she has been cheating on you, this person will scream, "How could you spy on me?" This cheater will then make you feel bad and guilty for violating his or her privacy, and all of a sudden you're made to feel that you have wronged him or her. When you try to tell this person that all this doesn't change the fact that he or she has cheated on you, he or she will just continue shaming you about your spying. Then the name-calling starts: "You're acting just like your overbearing mother." "You're being a bitch." "You're crazy!"

The Unfixables seem to come up with one trick or another to avoid answering any questions straight. They will talk around the issue, evade the issue entirely, pretend they don't understand what you're talking about, and just walk away claiming, "I can't take this anymore."

The Unfixables have many tricks up their sleeves, and when one trick fails, or when you see through the smoke and mirrors, they just pull another one out of left field. They always find a scapegoat to blame things on, or threaten to hurt you or ruin you, if you keep things up. They'll play on your every fear, and push every one of your crazy buttons. They'll threaten to abandon you, disown you, and humiliate you. They're sure to let you know that they'll throw you under the bus or kick you to the curb and never look back. They never play fair and will never settle for an eye for an eye. They will go after your right eye, your left arm, and your firstborn. They're the masters of emotional, psychological, and financial blackmail.

If all else fails, they will throw hissy fits and rage like lunatics. They know that one or all of the above tricks will usually get people to break down or back down.

The good news is that once the blinders are off and you see the man behind the curtain, any power these people once had over you, miraculously disappears.

Questions for Self-Analysis

1. Name a time when you enabled someone. What tactic did this person use to manipulate you? Did this person guilt you into helping? Did this person shame you, blame you, or name you as an accomplice?

2. Have you ever allowed a family member to steal an inheritance or rob from you? Did you just turn the other cheek and walk away?

3. Is it hard for you to walk away from family members, even after they've hurt you, lied to you, or betrayed you?

4. How many of *The Unfixables* are in your world right now?

5. After reading this book thus far, can you think of different strategies to deal with these people?

6. Are there some people in your life right now whom you may need to walk away from to ensure your own psychological, emotional, physical, or financial well-being?

Five

Your Fourth So-Called Good Trait:
Your Inability to Punish the Inner Circle
Or, I Let Everyone I Know Get Away with
Bloody Murder

In the end, we will remember not the words of our enemies, but the silence of our friends.

—Martin Luther King Jr.

Failing to Punish the Inner Circle

In the history of the world, the good people have rarely punished people they know, in other words, the inner circle. For instance, they've rarely had family members who have sexually abused them arrested, or sued siblings who have stolen their inheritances, or called the police on spouses who have beaten them.

Do you often ask yourself, *why is there so much injustice in this world?*

One reason is simply this: because "good people" don't punish the people they know. They have been brainwashed by so many tenets of organized religions that told them to give blind allegiance to family members and to the larger inner circle, which includes: employers, organizations that they belong to, the military, our governments, our churches, schools, and the like. They've been told to turn the other cheek; therefore, when people they've known and trusted have hurt them, betrayed them, stolen from them, and committed unspeakable acts against them, they've just walked away *without punishing or seeking justice.*

If you wish to have a world in which the molestation of children is a sin of the past and not one of the present, then this kind of thinking and behavior has got to stop. If a father, mother, brother, sister, aunt, uncle, grandparent, or any other family member molests another family member, then these people must be punished to the full extent of the law.

The true statistics concerning child sexual abuse are difficult, if not impossible to ascertain, since this type of crime is often not reported. After all, to do so would mean punishing family members, neighbors, so-called friends, clergy, coaches, and scout leaders—in other words, the inner circle. Additionally, the psychological mechanisms known as denial, suppression, and repression allow children to push the memories of these horrific acts out of their minds while they're ongoing. It may take decades for these memories to surface, if they ever do, further complicating our understanding of just how widespread this problem is. Sadly, many sexually abused people don't live to tell, since this kind of childhood abuse can lead to self-destructive and high-risk behaviors. What experts in this field do agree on is this: the incidence of child sexual abuse is far greater than what is actually reported to authorities.

For example, I have a client, Mary, who was molested by her father. When she told her mother about the incident, her mother accused her of being a liar and a slut and told her to never say such a horrible thing again about her father or else she would surely rot in hell one day. My client deeply repressed this memory, only to have it stirred up three decades later when her daughter told her, "Grandpa was touching me on my private parts." This time Mary didn't bother telling her mother what had happened. She immediately called the police and had her father arrested. Even though Mary was ostracized by the rest of her family, who all said she and her daughter were both crazy, she had no regrets about doing what she did. She said, "If I or someone else had called the police on him when I was a child, history may not have repeated itself. It's one thing to hurt me. It's an entirely different thing to hurt my child!"

You will read again and again in this book that you must love yourself as you love your own child. If it's not OK that someone did something to your child, then it's not OK that it has been done to you. It's your moral obligation to take appropriate action to rectify the situation.

As we learned in chapter 3, the true meaning of loyalty implies fidelity to a cause, a person, or group of people because: 1) those causes or those people have demonstrated themselves to be worthy of that sentiment, and 2) those causes or those people have an inherent sense of integrity, honesty, and truth.

Our first loyalty is and always shall be to Our Maker and our higher consciousness, with its moral compass guided by divine truth and not blind obedience to dogma.

If we give our loyalty to the wrong person or cause, and this sense of misplaced loyalty allows us to close our eyes to illegal or immoral actions, then this kind of reasoning will eventually result in disaster, betrayal, and ruin, not only for you, but for the world at large.

We must all learn to speak the truth. Unfortunately, sometimes, the truth can land us on a cross, as others—the inner circle, those people we once loved and trusted—turn on us, accusing us of being disloyal. We can take comfort knowing that this is our own Jesus moment, and ultimately we will be redeemed.

Stuffing Down Anger

The Great Enablers are not very good at expressing anger. In fact, they're often not in tune with anger itself. They've learned to stuff down unpleasant feelings, turn the other cheek, and do whatever they can do to keep peace at any price. You will read more about this tendency in chapter 7.

I often ask clients if they feel angry about painful situations they're currently experiencing, and they always look at me dumbfounded and answer "no." I then ask them, "If someone did these same horrendous things to your child would you be mad?" These same clients, without any hesitation, say that they would be "furious." I then ask them, "Why is it that everyone can dump on you, spit on you, steal from you, and do all kinds of unthinkable things to you, and yet you never feel angry? But, if these same crimes were committed upon your child, you would be mad as hell?" Again they stare at me, dumbfounded.

I then tell these clients, "In any given situation, if you would tell your beloved child to turn the other cheek and walk away in peace, then that's the correct way that you should respond to the situation. However, if you would tell your child to sue the bastard, then you must do the same!" This kind of anger is known as *divine anger*.

Henry David Thoreau as a Historic Example of Divine Anger in Action

...There are thousands who are in opinion opposed to slavery and to the war, who yet in effect do nothing to put an end to them.

—Henry David Thoreau

Henry David Thoreau was an American author, poet, naturalist, and Transcendentalist. Transcendentalism was a movement led by the poet, lecturer, and essayist, Ralph Waldo Emerson, which emphasized idealism and spiritualism over materialism. It's a philosophy deeply rooted in the belief that every human is a part of and an expression of humanity. Transcendentalists were asked to look inward to find moral truths and to trust their own consciences to be their infallible guides.

Thoreau was also a lifelong abolitionist, and his writings later influenced Mohandas Gandhi, Martin Luther King Jr., and Leo Tolstoy. Perhaps his most far-reaching piece of writing, published in 1849, was an essay entitled *Resistance to Civil Government*, which was later referred to as *Civil Disobedience*. He was motivated to write this piece because of his strong moral conviction that slavery was a great wrongdoing, and to voice his discontent against the Mexican-American war, which he believed to an imperialist war waged against Mexico and a brazen attempt by the United States to extend the boundaries of slavery. Back in 1846, Thoreau had symbolically protested this war by refusing to pay his Massachusetts poll tax, and had spent a night in jail meditating on and formulating many of the thoughts expressed in this essay.

This was a no-holds-barred, tell-it-like-it-is piece that argued that individuals cannot blindly obey governments and allow these man-made institutions to atrophy our consciences. He believed with all his being that American citizens should not allow or enable our government to commit acts of injustices against others. He was stressing that there is a higher law than a civil law, and that a higher law—one dictated by your own conscience—must be followed even if a penalty ensues.

What lessons can we learn from this free-spirited, intelligent, and moral man? We can learn to use our divine anger to change ourselves, others, and the world. We're asked to speak up and put our money where our mouths are. Yes, we may be jailed, ostracized, and crucified, but we're asked to rise above our fears, and to do this we must muster our courage and call upon Divine Providence for guidance.

Divine Anger: Knowing When to Turn the Tables

No one can hurt you without your permission.

—Mahatma Gandhi

First and foremost, *The Good-to-a-Fault People* of the world have to stop stuffing down their anger. *The Great Enablers* have come to believe that anger is not a nice emotion, and for this reason, they would rather deny, suppress, repress, and ignore their angry thoughts.

News flash: It's time for all the good people in the world to wake up and smell the coffee: anger is a valid emotion, and one that we must be in touch with. We're also going to have to stop seeing anger as a "bad" thing. I know for many of you this won't be easy! It may take a long while for you to stop thinking that anger is an ungodly emotion. When someone commits an injustice against us, morally or legally, then we must acknowledge the anger we feel. This kind of righteous anger is *divine anger*. This is the kind of anger that was referred to in the New Testament (Ephesians 4:26–27). "Be angry, and don't sin. Don't let the sun go down on your wrath, and don't give place to the devil."

What does divine anger imply? How can we be angry but not sinful? These are the big moral dilemmas each and every one of us faces each and every day of our lives.

Most of us have never been taught godly ways of expressing anger. We haven't learned to say what we mean and mean what we say without being mean about it. We've been taught to stuff down our feelings so much that by the time push comes to shove and we let out this emotion, we do it in highly destructive, explosive, and over-the-top ways. This kind of expression of anger usually backfires on us, and we come across looking like lunatics. This is *mortal anger*.

Properly executed, divine anger becomes an instrument that can lead to God's righteousness on earth, whereas mortal anger can only lead to heartbreak, bloodshed, vengeance, and more bloodshed. We're asked to be God's instruments of peace, through the vehicle of divine anger. Properly thought-out, planned, and executed, this kind of divine anger becomes a reflection of God, and we execute the kind of justice that God would expect us to do. If we do our parts to seek justice in a fair and moral manner, then we can expect the universe to do its part in bringing about a state of divine retribution. The popular expression "revenge is a dish best serve cold" reminds us to not act rashly in the heat of the moment, but to wait until we can react in a calm and rational way in our quest for justice for all.

Mortal anger is powered by fear and by the scarcity principle, which gives humans the false belief that there isn't enough abundance or love on this planet for all of us.

This creates a dog-eat-dog mentality in which humans revert back to their animal nature. Mortal anger is greedy, selfish, harshly critical, and narcissistic, and this thinking translates into actions that reflect that each man must be out for himself. Mortal anger is based on the kind of loving that is very conditional in nature. In other words, I love you if you do as I say, behave as I tell you, and do what I want you to do. Mortal anger is unfair, impulsive, intolerant, and highly judgmental. Mortal anger judges not only the actions of people, but it judges the people as well. Mortal anger is filled with hubris, and because of this haughty pride, all efforts are aimed at saving face. The proverb "Before you embark on a journey of revenge, dig two graves" warns us to think carefully and act judiciously in our dealings with others, so that we may live to tell our tale of justice done.

Divine anger is powered by our love of God, self-love, love for others, and love for all of humanity. Divine anger is based on *agape* love, which is the unconditional love of all of humankind and of all of God's creation. Therefore, divine anger is fair, patient, tolerant, and nonjudgmental. Divine anger is inspired by people's unjust, unkind, or unfair actions, and it's these actions that are being judged, not the people. Divine anger, by its very nature, brings us to a mind-set of humility, and this humility allows us to be compassionate and understanding of others. Divine anger is egalitarian in nature; therefore, when we are in a state of divine anger, we don't find some people more lovable and worthy of fair treatment because of their race, creed, or color. Instead, we see that every human, by the very fact of his or her humanity, is entitled to fair and just treatment. Because divine anger is patient, this patience allows us to wait when necessary to win over our opponents, and it allows us to be tolerant and merciful in the meantime. Mahatma Gandhi epitomized this kind of thinking when he said, "Hate the sin. Love the sinner."

Characteristics of Mortal Anger—Anger without Conscience or Consciousness

1. Mortal anger is fear-based; therefore, when push comes to shove, anything goes. This kind of anger is out of control, filled with outbursts, screaming, shouting, expletives, temper tantrums, and impulsive violence characterized by hair-trigger reactions and temporary insanity.

2. Mortal anger is childlike in its need for instant justice. We've all seen these hotheaded people in action, and it's not a pretty picture. These people are all for taking an eye for an eye in an instant, and giving little thought to the fact that too much of these kinds of actions would create a world of regretful blind people. An example of this kind of anger can be seen on our highways and byways, and we refer to this as "road rage."

3. Mortal anger is crazy anger filled with vengeance and retaliation, without any regard for later consequences. Television loves to show this kind of blind rage and violence on an hourly basis, even though numerous studies have linked violence in the media to the increase in violence in the outside world.

4. Mortal anger is taking justice into your own hands, even if it means placing bombs in a public place and killing innocent people in the name of your cause. Think of all the suicide bombers and of the Boston Marathon explosions on April 15, 2013, which killed and maimed so many innocent bystanders.

5. Mortal anger can create vigilantes who truly feel that the end justifies the means.

6. Mortal anger is big anger and seeks to be larger than life in its display. The more people hurt and the larger the media coverage the better.

7. Mortal anger is one-sided, myopic, and self-serving.

8. Mortal anger is unrelenting and without end. It's highly destructive and spares no one. It takes prisoners and will destroy anyone or anything that gets in its way.

9. Mortal anger is fueled by ignorance, prejudice, and a need to oppress others to ensure one's own superiority.

10. Mortal anger is highly destructive to all parties involved, since it is vigilant and militant.

11. Those who are proponents of mortal anger walk in the footsteps of the likes of men who are guilty of massive crimes against humanity—Hitler (Germany), Stalin (USSR), Mussolini (Italy), Mao Tse-Tung (China)—and of self-appointed vigilantes such as Timothy McVeigh (Oklahoma City) and Tamerlan Tsarnaev and Dzhokhar Tsarnaev (Boston); and other senseless killers, including: Adam Lanza (Newtown, CT), James Holmes (Aurora, CO), and Eric David Harris and Dylan Bennet Klebold (Columbine, CO). The list of angry killers from the past could fill the rest of this book and way beyond. As technology and easy access to information concerning the building of weapons of mass destruction grows, I shudder to think of the death toll in the future if we as a species do not evolve toward a collective state of higher consciousness.

Characteristics of Divine Anger—Anger Driven by Conscience and Executed with Consciousness

1. Divine anger is love-based. Courage fuels this kind of anger and keeps us steadfast in our missions.

2. Divine anger has respect for the law and tries to work within the context of the law to achieve its ultimate goal, which is justice. Superseding legal laws are moral laws, as was pointed out in the previous section about Henry David Thoreau.

3. If a law is unjust or amoral, such as the laws in the United States that once allowed slavery and discrimination against blacks, then we must work within the context of existing laws to change unjust ones. There's a time for peace and a time for war, and sometimes a war becomes a necessary evil, a way to a means, to see that justice is done. Our own American Civil War was a reflection of this thinking, as was World War II, a war that was necessary to end Nazism, Fascism, Japanese militarism, and the resultant consequence of these three oppressive forces—genocide. The thinking "My country right or wrong" has to be reevaluated to be more along the thinking "My country—right the wrongs!"

4. Divine anger is controlled anger. It's not about outbursts, explosions, and tirades. Divine anger is strategic, calm, patient, and thoughtful.

5. Divine anger "walks a mile in my shoes." This kind of anger is founded in truth, fairness, and justice for all. Divine anger sees the whole picture, the whole truth, and nothing but the truth.

6. Divine anger does not judge people, but it does judge their actions, and holds them fully accountable for these actions.

7. Divine anger can be compromising when necessary, but divine anger does not compromise on the core moral issues, in which there can be no compromise. It's a lot like the expression "you can't be a little bit pregnant." You're either with child or you aren't. When it comes to sexual abuse or violence committed against innocent human beings, a line of zero tolerance must be drawn in the sand.

8. Divine anger asks that we confront the person or persons who have hurt us. Firstly, we're asked to do this as quietly and discreetly as we can. We do not seek to publicly humiliate or castrate others. We save the heavy artillery for when these people give us no other choice.

9. Divine anger recognizes that there will be instances when we have done all that we could do morally and legally to right a wrong, and yet, injustice appears to have won. At these times, we're asked to accept that divine justice will intervene, in this lifetime or in the afterlife, and we must find solace in that knowledge. We must leave these times to the future wrath of God and go in peace, knowing that we have done all that we can for now.

10. Divine anger is ultimately altruistic and constructive.

11. When executing divine anger, you walk in the divine footsteps of Jesus, Buddha, Gandhi, Thoreau, and Martin Luther King Jr.

Knowing How and When to Punish Others

Basically, any time someone acts in a morally or legally offensive way to us, we're asked to love ourselves the way we love or would love our own children. If you would tell your child to turn the other cheek, then that is how you would rightfully respond to that particular situation. If you would tell your child to sue the bastard, then that is what you yourself should do under the circumstances. Again, I can't stress this truism enough!

The world will become a fairer and more just place when each of us deals appropriately with people who have hurt us, stolen from us, or acted in an illegal or immoral way to us. Sometimes, just cutting them out of our lives is enough punishment. Other times, it calls for harsher actions, such as: having them arrested, suing them, having them removed from their positions, and that kind of thing.

There will be times in your life when you'll be asked to be the leader, the one holding the moral compass, the conscience of others, even if you're seemingly the only one with the courage to do so. Through your righteous words, deeds, and actions you will, in due time, become a beacon of light for others to see. All of us will have our Jesus moments—those trying times where we feel crucified and alone. At these times we must pray for backup, and hope that others will join us and form an army of supporters.

Hitler and Gandhi as Twentieth-Century Examples of Mortal Anger versus Divine Anger: Two Diametrically Opposed Reactions to Prejudice

It's hard to believe that Adolph Hitler and Mohandas K. Gandhi walked the earth in the same time continuum. Each of these men dealt with prejudice in diametrically opposed ways. One man, Hitler, used mortal anger, with all its violence and bloodshed, in a highly destructive way to imprison and destroy people; and the other man, Gandhi, used the power of divine anger and nonviolence to liberate and free others.

There are so many theories and opposing theories as to what may have caused Hitler to become a rabid anti-Semite, but what we can all agree upon is this: he was a highly prejudiced man, with obsessions and delusions that centered on the hatred and destruction of the Jewish people. The Nazi party held the ideology, which was based on those of the German social Darwinists of the late nineteenth century, that human beings could be classified into different races, and that only the fittest would and should survive. The Nazis defined Judaism not as a religion, but as a race. The Nazis further believed that the German "Aryan" race was superior to all others. Therefore, they came to believe that it was their moral obligation to see that this race survived and evolved to become the supreme race, and that it was their divine obligation to exterminate any inferior races. This ideology not only allowed for, but encouraged, the premeditated mass murder of six million Jews, and millions and millions of other innocent people of all colors and creeds.

Hitler is the quintessential example of *The Unfixables*.

Mohandas K. Gandhi, known as the Mahatma, which means Great Soul, experienced racial discrimination when he went to South Africa to practice law. The ruling white Boers discriminated against all people of color, including Indians. Gandhi later became an outspoken critic of South African discrimination policies and eventually landed in jail for disobeying what he believed to be unjust laws. While in jail he read Thoreau's essay *Civil Disobedience,* which had a profound and life-changing influence on him. He began to formulate his theory of nonviolent protest against injustice, adopting the term *civil disobedience* to describe his strategies. Later on, he began using the term *Satyagraha,* or *Soul Force,* which included in its name truth and love, the two most powerful forces in the universe. Gandhi learned to harness the power of divine anger, which is peaceful, calm, and strategic, to bring about change. Years later, he would use this same ideology to help win Indian independence.

Gandhi is the quintessential example of *The Enlightened Ones.*

Gandhi's Two Letters to Hitler

Gandhi wrote two letters appealing to Hitler to end his evil ways. The first letter, written on July 23, 1939, was a plea for Hitler, who was the one person in the world who could prevent a war, to please do so.

The second letter was written on Christmas Eve, 1940. This was a no-holds-barred letter asking Hitler to stop the scientific war machine that he had created. Gandhi explains in the opening of the letter how he had worked for the past thirty-three years to befriend all of humanity, regardless of race, color, or creed. I could only imagine Hitler's rapid rise in blood pressure when he read that paragraph.

Later he boldly calls Hitler's actions "...monstrous and unbecoming of human dignity..." Talk about mustering up courage! When Hitler read the words "...the humiliation of Czechoslovakia, the rape of Poland...," one can only wonder what hatred must have welled up in him toward the brazen pacifist from India.

Gandhi also discussed India's own need to resist British imperialism. He states, "Our resistance to it does not mean harm to the British people. We seek to convert them, not to defeat them on the battle-field." Once again, you can only wonder what thoughts went through Hitler's head when he read this. Did he laugh at Gandhi's childlike belief that he could effect change with an unarmed revolt?

Gandhi also acknowledged in that letter that no spoliator could accomplish his ends without some degree of cooperation from the victims.

Gandhi also let Hitler know that the Indian people had found in nonviolence a force that when organized could match itself against the most violent forces in the universe.

This was a brave and heartfelt letter. Unfortunately, it did little to stop this mad man.

Gandhi, One of *The Enlightened Ones*, as an Example of Divine Anger in Action

It is my conviction that nothing enduring can be built upon violence.

—Mahatma Gandhi

1. Divine anger is patient—patient enough to allow you to wait to win over your opponents. Gandhi employed nonviolent methods such as noncooperation with an unjust system, boycotts, peaceful demonstrations, and hunger strikes to get his message across and then waited patiently for change to come.

2. He tried to appeal to the good in others and to hook their higher consciousness. He worked hard to avoid bringing men to their animal nature by being disrespectful or violent, or by uttering threats, bullying, or name calling. He addressed his second letter to Hitler "Dear Friend." In the opening paragraph of the letter he wrote, "That I address you as a friend is no formality. I own no foes." He then went on to say that he was in the business of befriending all of mankind, regardless of race, creed, or color.

3. He always tried to walk a mile in the other person's shoes and to understand the other person's point of view. Divine anger is fair to all parties involved, and Gandhi states in his letter to Hitler, "We have no doubt about your bravery or devotion to your fatherland."

4. Gandhi expresses his anger at a man's actions and not at the person. He states in his letter to Hitler, "...Your own writings and pronouncements and those of your friends and admirers leave no room

for doubt that many of your actions are monstrous and unbecoming of human dignity..."

5. Gandhi was free from the sin of self-serving narcissism. His cause was larger than anything he wanted for himself. He wanted to free his people and all people from the wrath of prejudice. Hitler, on the other hand, believed that he came from a superior Aryan race, and that the annihilation of other races, which he deemed inferior, was not only his right, but his mission. Gandhi wrote in his letter to Hitler, "... Such are your humiliation of Czechoslovakia, the rape of Poland... I am aware that your view of life regards such spoliations as virtuous acts. But we have been taught from childhood to regard them as acts degrading to humanity."

6. Gandhi once said, "The world has enough for everyone's need, but not enough for everyone's greed." He worked tirelessly in his life to liberate people from the bottomless pit of desire, which is all-consuming and insatiable. Hitler had an appetite for power and control that knew no limits, and all of his actions fed, but never satisfied, that unrelenting monster.

7. Gandhi's actions were the living embodiment of divine anger. He was free of envy and jealousy; therefore, liberated from the life-destroying emotion known as hate. In his letter to Hitler he stated, "We resist British Imperialism no less than Nazism. If there is a difference, it is in degree... Our resistance does not mean harm to the British people." As we all know, Hitler was filled with hatred, and a great deal of this hatred was fueled by envy and jealousy. He both envied and hated the Jews. His hatred drove him to create technology with the sole purpose of destroying human life, and anyone who got in his way would be destroyed as well.

8. Gandhi's divine anger was the voice of freedom ringing for all people. Gandhi believed in democracy, whereas Hitler's mortal anger was fueled by his belief in dictatorship, and had the ominous sound of machine guns, grenades, bombs, and other weapons of mass destruction.

9. Gandhi was always guided by his higher consciousness and his divine conscience; therefore, he sought to inspire love and respect in people, especially in those who opposed him. He addressed the differences in ideology between himself and his opponents, but he never attacked individuals. He didn't want to make enemies, but rather, he focused on coming to common ground; and in the name of humanity, he sought to make friends of his opponents. He never wanted to cause bloodshed, believing that all life was sacred. Hitler had no love for humanity and only believed that certain people had a right to inhabit this earth. Gandhi's enemies were the errors in thinking and actions of his opponents, but not the opponents themselves. Gandhi was fighting what he believed to be the enemy of all humankind: ignorance, colonialism, poverty, racism, and the like. He was not fighting people. He had a deep reverence for of all God's creatures. He didn't view the British people as his enemy, but believed their colonial rule was the enemy. Gandhi sought to never hurt, maim, or injure even one British person; he only wished for them to leave India to independently rule itself. Hitler's mortal anger brought out the worst in people; therefore, he made many enemies. Indeed, his actions led to World War II, a war in which upward of fifty million people lost their lives.

10. Gandhi's higher consciousness thinking strived to bring out the best in people, whereas Hitler's actions brought out the worst in people. Divine anger

seeks positive change, while mortal anger seeks to oppress others at any cost. Divine anger is focused on a person's thoughts and actions and not directed at the person, whereas mortal anger is waged against both a person's thoughts and actions and at the person as well. Gandhi once said, "An eye for an eye will only make the whole world blind."

11. Gandhi's divine anger epitomized *agape* love in action. *Agape* love is altruistic, unconditional love for humankind and all God's creations. *Agape* love gives reverence to all things. This is the kind of love that is spoken of in the traditional religious texts. *Agape* love is kind, patient, tolerant, and nonjudgmental. This is the kind of love that God has for all of us. *Agape* love asks not "What can you do for me?" but "What can I do for you?" *Agape* love is a very egalitarian way of loving, for we are not supposed to find some people more lovable and worthy than others. For example, in our Judeo-Christian culture, it seems perfectly acceptable to many people to find Muslims unlovable. In practicing *agape* love, we come to realize that the external differences are inconsequential. All paths lead to God, and we come to love all human beings regardless of race, color, or creed.

12. *Agape* love asks that we love all humanity, and this implies that we must love our enemies as well. This is never easy, and in many cases, never possible. Yet, *agape* love is patient, so patient that it waits to win over our opponents, and it helps us to be tolerant, kind, nonjudgmental, merciful, and forgiving in the meantime. Gandhi respected all religions and all races, and sought a world filled with peace and prejudice toward none. Hitler used propaganda to manipulate the German people to believe in a collective delusion that they were the chosen Aryan race, who were destined to govern the world, and

that the Jews had to be exterminated to execute this grand and divine mission.

13. Divine anger strives toward peaceful resolution of differences and reverts to violence only as a last resort, when push turns to shove. In writing to Hitler, Gandhi tried to explain that the Indian people's resistance toward British Imperialism did not mean harm to the British people. He stated, "We seek to convert them, not to defeat them on the battlefield." Mortal anger is aggressive anger in which the end justifies the means. Hitler once said, "The very first essential for success is a perpetually constant and regular employment of violence."

14. Divine anger is tolerant and slow to boil. It's based in truth and justice. Mortal anger is intolerant and acts as both the judge and the jury. Hitler believed in using any ploy and any lie to manipulate others and to stir anger in them, so that they would follow his evil plan. "Make the lie big, make it simple, keep saying it, and eventually they will believe it." That Hitler quote summed up his method of brainwashing the German people. Mortal anger needs an army to back it, and will use any means to gather that army. Gandhi believed that "even if you are a minority of one, the truth is the truth." Divine anger stands strong alone, doesn't waver from its course, and doesn't back down in fear.

15. Divine anger is righteous and rational anger. It's well-thought-out through self-reflection and deep inner searching. It doesn't need instant gratification, and waits for the right time and place to express itself. Although it is steadfast and unwavering, once it begins its course, it rarely resorts to actions in which the end justifies the means. Only in the most extreme cases, and matters of life and death, does mortal anger every resort to these kinds of tactics.

Hitler, One of *The Unfixables*, as an Example of Mortal Anger in Action

Demoralize the enemy from within with surprise, terror, sabotage, assassination. This is the war of the future.

—Adolf Hitler

1. Mortal anger is always obsessive by nature, and "the end justifies the means" is a guiding principle. Hitler's fanatical belief that it was his mission to see that the master race inherit the earth allowed him to justify any and all methods to see that this plan was executed.
2. All mortal anger is aggressive in its need to be right. It's a "my way or the highway" kind of thinking. In Hitler's world, there was no discussion, no democracy, and zero tolerance for dissenters or others who were deemed undesirable. Hitler authorized the mass extermination of at least eleven million people, including Jews, other minorities, homosexuals, priests, pastors, the disabled, anyone who voiced protest, Jehovah's Witnesses, Roma gypsies, and resisters. From this example, you can plainly see that mortal anger seeks to destroy its enemy and to annihilate anyone or anything that stands in its way.
3. Mortal anger seeks absolute power. Hitler didn't want to give voting rights to the masses, since he believed in a totalitarian government ruled by a dictator.
4. Mortal anger is always a one-sided view of the world, and those people who subscribe to this kind of anger are highly narcissistic, judgmental, maniacal, intolerant, selfish, self-serving, arrogant, and egotistical. To them, the end justifies the means, and lying,

manipulation, bloodshed, bullying, screaming, and intimidation tactics are justified accordingly.

5. Mortal anger can be motivated by jealousy and by envying and coveting what others have. Mortal anger is blinding anger, and in that blindness, denial, suppression, rationalization, displacement, and any and all psychological defense systems are utilized to motivate the individual or group and keep them on a self-serving path. Hitler's treatment of the Jews can be viewed as a historical example of prejudice inspired by envy. Prior to his rise to power, many German people were already anti-Semites, and some of these prejudicial feelings were partly based on envy rooted in the perception that the Jews in Germany had too much economic power and cultural influence in Germany. Hitler capitalized on these feelings and was able to manipulate the German people to see Jews as a threat to Germany.

6. Mortal anger can express itself in vigilante behaviors. This kind of anger is rationalized by the self-serving belief that it's an individual's or group's moral duty, their mission, to set things right by any means necessary. Hitler's rise to power is a great example of vigilantism in action. Propaganda and violence were his main instruments used to control others. Hitler had a singleness of purpose: to establish the Third Reich as an all-powerful German nation. Hitler believed that he had been chosen by Providence to accomplish this great mission, and that the Jews had to be eliminated before this vision could be brought to fruition. Consequently, Hitler's mortal anger, waged at anyone or anything that stood in the way of this mission, knew no bounds. Varying degrees of violence are always employed by vigilantes. Bombing, burning down businesses or buildings, and maiming or killing people are par for the course. During the early years

of the civil rights movement, lynching was one of the most common forms of vigilantism in the United States. Vigilantism has been part of the antiabortion movement, and violence committed against individuals or clinics that provided abortions have included destruction of property by arson, bombing, or vandalism; and crimes against doctors, nurses, or the staff of abortion clinics have involved kidnapping, stalking, harassment, assaults, and even murder.

How to Use Your Divine Anger to Effect Change in People or Circumstances

Remember that in any situation, it is best to start with the least aggressive method, if you can, and then start pulling out the heavy artillery, if you must!

1. Tell people what they have done in as private a manner as possible and try reasoning with them.
2. A well-written letter can do the trick in many cases.
3. File a lawsuit against them.
4. Have them arrested.
5. Have them removed from their positions.
6. Cut them out of your life.

Something Good Comes from Something Bad

Interestingly enough, because of Hitler and the profound effect that World War II had on the British economy, Britain was forced to leave India in 1947. Believe me, it was never Hitler's intent to liberate anyone. He was a conqueror and sought world domination. Had the war gone differently, India might have fallen into the hands of even worse oppressors: the Nazi Regime, the Fascists, or perhaps the militant Japanese.

These regimes would have had zero tolerance for civil disobedience, and any followers would have been gassed or, more likely, executed on the spot. Under these totalitarian regimes, Gandhi wouldn't have been able to practice peaceful resistance, the way he was capable of doing under the more civilized British colonialism. We can only speculate that, had the war gone differently and Gandhi had tried to practice civil disobedience under a dictatorial regime, he would have come to realize that when you're dealing with humans who have descended to their animal nature, reasoning, letter writing, and quiet protests would get you nowhere, except to an early grave.

I equate mortal anger with the behavior of a rabid animal. Even if you had raised a beloved pet to be gentle and obedient, if it became rabid because it had been bitten by another rabid animal, all your soft talk and reasoning would not keep you from being eaten alive by this mad animal that could no longer be reasoned with. As that rabid animal lunged at you, you would have to practice self-defense, and in defending yourself, this animal might very well be killed. In any and all cases, divine anger always uses violence as a last resort.

Questions for Self-Analysis

1. Were you brought up by a parent or parents who employed mortal anger techniques in raising you? For example, did they beat you, bully you, scream at you, degrade and insult you, and lead you to believe

that you would lose their love if you didn't see things their way or act in accordance with their beliefs?

2. Can you remember a time when your anger took on the characteristics of mortal anger? How did that work out for you? If you could do it all again, would you react differently?

3. Can you remember a time, when someone's mortal anger frightened you into doing things or acting in a way that you're not proud of?

4. Think about a particularly trying situation that is going on in your life right now. Have you been practicing mortal anger techniques? Why not try practicing divine anger techniques and see how that changes things? Write down your strategy for handling this situation in a more karmically correct manner, utilizing the techniques given in this chapter.

Six

Your Fifth So-Called Good Trait:
You Forgive Too Easily and Too Often
Or, I Turn the Other Cheek So Often That I'm
Slapped Silly

Then Peter came and said to him, "Lord how often shall my brother sin against me, and I forgive him? Until seven times?"

Jesus said to him, "I don't tell you until seven times, but, until seventy times seven."

—Matthew 18:21–22

Wow, seventy times seven times sounds like an awful lot of times to forgive someone, and indeed it is; but more importantly, this rule of thumb sets a limit to just how many times we need to forgive someone before we can throw in the towel. Jesus didn't say, "You forgive countless times, or a gazillion times"; he gave a finite number: 490 times. For the most part, when we are dealing with one of *The Unfixables* we have forgiven him or her that many times in a year or less!

When Jesus walked the earth, many scholars believe he spoke Aramaic. The Aramaic word to forgive literally means to "untie." Therefore, what Jesus was telling you to do to free yourself from your nemesis was simply this: you must untie the psychological and emotional rope that binds you to this person or to the situation. When we haven't forgiven someone, we are energetically bound to this person. These invisible cords are just as binding as any chains, and by forgiving someone, we free ourselves from the bondage of hatred, resentment, and revenge. Our ill feelings keep us tied to those who have hurt and betrayed us. When we let go of our past hurts, we are free to move on with our own lives. Until we forgive our enemies, we are enmeshed with them, tangled in their webs of deceit and pain. Forgiveness cuts these strangulating cords and frees us to walk away in peace.

Forgiveness holds the key to unchaining the pain that binds us to someone or something we would rather leave behind.

What Does It Mean to Forgive?

Forgive—how does the dictionary define this word? *Forgive* is a verb first and foremost, so it is an action word. Most dictionaries that I consulted basically defined the verb *forgive* this way: to stop feeling resentment or anger toward another or toward others for an offense committed against you, for a flaw this person or these people possess, or for a mistake this person or these people made.

Forgiveness of others is part of *The Great Enablers'* very nature. However, they forgive others too easily, too often, and too quickly, without doing the necessary steps that true forgiveness demands.

Most of us say we forgive long before the anger or the resentment has subsided. Most of the time, ***The Great Enablers*** deny, suppress, or repress angry feelings, thereby deluding themselves and others into thinking that they've done the real inner homework necessary to forgive another.

Most of us have no idea what forgiveness really means. We still go by the childhood notion that when someone says "I'm sorry," they mean it, and we have to accept that, and in turn, forget about what was done. This is not forgiveness: this is denial.

Remember: The road to forgiveness is long and steep, winding and weary. Traveled correctly, with an army of angels and God by your side, it's a freedom trail. Wrongly traversed, it's the road to ruin for all parties involved.

What Forgiveness Doesn't Mean

Most of us have been taught in grade school and in Sunday school that to forgive others means that we let them off the hook for their offenses simply because they have uttered the words "I'm sorry" or "Forgive me." We're then expected to keep them in our lives or be friendly to them, as if nothing ever happened, and as if they never hurt us.

God does want us to forgive people, but not necessarily their actions. If these actions are hurtful, abusive, threatening, annoying, and destructive to our mental, emotional, physical, psychological, and spiritual selves, then we have the God-given right to stop trusting this person or these people and to stop allowing them to be in our lives.

Forgiveness doesn't mean that people get off the hook without being accountable for their actions. Yes, people are expected to ask for forgiveness, but they must also be held accountable for what they did, and they're expected to make amends or offer compensation for these actions. Most importantly, they must come to the full understanding that these kinds of behaviors or actions are never to occur again.

Furthermore, you can forgive someone without forgiving what he or she did to you. This gives you the right to walk away from that person and never look back, particularly when you know in your heart of hearts that if you keep this person in your life he or she will only hurt you time and time again.

Forgiveness happens in due time. Forgiveness is a long process, not accomplished by uttering "I'm sorry," as if these words are some kind of magic wand that makes all the pain and hurt disappear.

Yes, it's still possible to forgive those who don't repent. That kind of forgiveness implies that we don't judge the people themselves, but rather, it's their actions we're judging to be unkind, cruel, unjust, mean, hateful, greedy, etc. In no way does forgiving someone obligate you to continue having a relationship in the future with this unremorseful person, who would just go on hurting you from now until doomsday. This is what Jesus meant when he uttered this cry from the cross, "Father, forgive them, for they know not what they do" (Luke 23:34).

False forgiveness or "narcissistic forgiveness" is pretending to forgive and putting on a show about how we have forgiven someone so that others will find us righteous and religious, or so that others will like us or not judge us to be unlikable.

Forgiveness does not mean forgetting. *The Great Enablers* have very short memories for abuse, and they make a lot of excuses for abuse. When we forget what people have done in the past, it allows them to hurt us again and again in the future. The old adage "Fool me once, shame on you; fool me twice, shame on me" reminds us to protect ourselves in the future from people who have proven to be untrustworthy in the past. We need to learn how to *forgive and remember,* so that these injustices will never repeat themselves. The next time that you're tempted to just *forgive and forget,* remember that this can only be possible if this person is genuinely remorseful and fully intends to never commit that kind of indiscretion again.

Forgiveness has to be a conscious decision to let go of feelings of resentment and thoughts of vengeance. Before this can happen, justice must be done; then forgiveness will follow.

True forgiveness is not just a shift in our thinking; it's a closing of a wound to our hearts, minds, bodies, and souls. This takes time, justice, and the making of amends. Once these things have taken place, then forgiveness becomes a conscious act of moving beyond victim consciousness toward cosmic consciousness, in which we learn that it's all good, if we and others learn the right lessons from that experience.

—⁂—

Remember: One of the hardest things that you'll ever have to do is to learn to forgive the unforgivable. This can only be achieved through righteous actions, justice properly executed, and the grace of God that follows.

—⁂—

What Forgiveness Isn't

1. **Forgiveness isn't denial.** Denying that someone has done something unjust, unfair, or unkind to us does not mean it didn't happen. It just allows this person to continue to do the same kind of horrific things over and over without suffering any consequences. True forgiveness always recognizes the enormity of

the wrongdoing and never tries to minimize or rationalize away the wrongdoing.

2. **Forgiveness is not forgetting what was done to us.** *The Great Enablers* seem to have an enormous capacity for forgetting injustices committed against them. We tend to deny that any wrongdoings are ever done to us, thanks to the brainwashing we received all of our lives from our family members, churches, temples, and schools that we should just "get over it," or "don't tattle on others," or "turn the other cheek," or "forgive and forget." Just remember that if we forget, rewrite, or deny the past, this kind of thinking will allow the same kind of injustices to perpetuate without end. We can use the Holocaust as an example. We must remember what happened to eleven million people so that it never happens again.

3. **Forgiveness is not blind, empty words uttered.** Just because someone says "I'm sorry" doesn't mean we just say "OK, I forgive you." Saying that you forgive someone is not the same as forgiveness.

4. **Forgiveness doesn't mean that you have to reconcile with someone.** Reconciliation is a two-way street. It isn't up to the offended party to let bygones be bygones, if the offending party has no intention of changing. Reconciliation must be earned by the guilty party through words and deeds. A sincere apology, in which that person fully acknowledges the wrongdoing, is the first step toward allowing this person back into your life. Secondly, there must be a heartfelt promise to never repeat the offense. Thirdly, steps must be taking to make full amends for past mistakes. Amends might come in the form of a monetary settlement, or it could mean that this person must go to therapy or jail, or do whatever it takes to right the past wrongs. Even after all is said and done, reconciling with this person, no matter

how much he or she repents, is ultimately up to you. You can forgive someone, but—no matter how well-intentioned this person may appear—if in your soul-searching evaluations, you come to believe that this person still holds great potential to hurt and betray you in the future, you have the right to walk away. This is an act of self-love. Your intention in walking away is not to hurt this person, but to protect yourself or others from being hurt by this person again. Just know that you can forgive someone without continuing the relationship, and certainly you are expected to cut this person out of your life to protect you and yours from any future harm.

5. **Forgiveness is not acceptance of wrongdoings or wrong behavior.** Forgiveness does not imply that you condone or excuse the offending actions. Forgiveness doesn't mean you let someone off the hook. Forgiveness means people must suffer the consequences of their actions. This may teach them how to behave better in the future. *The Unfixables* probably won't learn to be better human beings, but they might stop doing bad things just because they fear punishment.

What Forgiveness Is

1. **Forgiveness recognizes the wrongdoer's intentions.** Some pain is caused by an accident, and these actions must be evaluated fairly and with compassion for all parties involved. We must still make amends for the accidental harm we may have caused others—that's what insurance is for—and furthermore, the punishment must be fair and fit the crime. Still other pain is intentionally inflicted. Whether these

actions are done subconsciously or consciously or are premeditated or committed impulsively must also be evaluated. Intentional pain must be dealt with much more harshly. For instance, making an honest mistake or misjudgment when driving that results in injury or death to another must still be amended for, but the punishment doesn't usually involve jailing the person. However, the same injury that's a result of someone driving under the influence must be dealt with as a criminal case.

2. **Forgiveness is only possible if we come to the place of understanding why someone may have done what they did to us.** This understanding can bring us to a place of compassion. For example, we can come to forgive the pedophile, but not the sins this pedophile committed, when we learn what was done in the past to this person that caused him or her to react this way. We can forgive those who did not protect us from this person when we come to understand that they were incapable of seeing such evil. Sometimes people who have been sexually abused as children have so deeply repressed and suppressed what happened that they're incapable of seeing the same kind of thing when it's being done right under their noses.

The Forgiveness Process—A Step-by-Step Approach

1. **First you must become fully conscious of what has been done to you.** You must rip off the blinders and throw away the rose-colored glasses that have allowed you to go into a state of deep denial. You will then stop ignoring injustices that are presently

being done to you, and you will effectively deal with injustices that have been committed against you in the past.

2. **You confront the person or persons who have hurt or betrayed you.**

3. **You then allow some time for those who have offended you to make amends.**

4. **You take steps to see that justice is done.** This may mean filing a lawsuit, having these people arrested, or taking any other moral, yet, necessary steps to see that these people are held accountable for their actions.

5. **Once you have done all that you can to see that these people are held accountable, regardless of the outcome, you are free to walk away in peace.** You will find inner peace in just knowing that you've done all that you can at the present time to rectify the situation. You're then asked to give these people up to God and walk away in peace, knowing that the law of Karma will ultimately right this wrong.

6. **In some cases, you will have to forgive yourself for allowing yourself to be hurt or betrayed by these people.** This is what we ask for when praying "... and forgive us our trespasses as we forgive those who trespass against us..." When children are abused, they truly have been victimized, and they must forgive themselves for being young and vulnerable, but they must also know that they were not responsible for the misguided behaviors of others. Children can be victims; grown-ups cannot be victims, unless they allow themselves to be. Learn to hold yourself accountable for your part in allowing situations to happen. Examine your own personality traits that left you vulnerable to an abusive person or situation. Why didn't you see the writing on the wall? Did you ignore your gut feelings? Look back and try to see

if there were any red flags that you ignored. Could you have stopped these actions sooner? Vow to move away from victim consciousness. *Remember that no one can use or abuse you without your permission.* Learn all you can from this experience so that you will never be fooled or taken advantage of again. Bless this experience because you have learned and grown from it; therefore, it's all good. **The Great Enablers** tend to forgive others too quickly, and yet they seem to have great difficulty in forgiving themselves. The karmic lesson in this situation is simple: you need to learn how to forgive yourself!

7. **You may now forgive the person or persons, but you are not asked to forgive the actions.** Forgiveness doesn't mean that you go into a state of denial as to what was done unto you or unto others, and it doesn't minimize these injustices. To continue to stay in a state of resentment or obsessing about seeking revenge will keep you feeling victimized. Once you forgive the person or persons, you're free to stop living in victim consciousness. Letting go of your angry feelings releases you from the control the offending party or parties have had on you, and you regain your personal power again.

8. **Remember: forgiveness does not mean you have to reconcile with these people.** In many cases, to allow **The Unfixables** back into your life would only give them other opportunities to hurt you. Forgiveness merely allows you to walk away guilt-free and in peace.

9. **You need to stop talking about what was done to you.** When people are in a state of pain, talk therapy helps, and you can engage in talk therapy just by telling someone you trust—a lover, friend, or family member—what happened. There is a point, however, where retelling this tale over and over again only

keeps it alive and keeps it in the present moment. There comes a time when you just have to stop obsessing about past hurts, and for the sake of all the people in your life who are sick and tired of listening to this litany, you just have to let it go. Obsessing about past hurts can lead to feelings of mortal anger, and that is never good.

10. **We then need to bless those who have trespassed against us by wishing them well, and just let go and let God handle the rest.**

Seeking to Forgive Those Who Have Crossed Over to the Other Side

Dying ends a life, but not our relationship with the deceased person. If you've been hurt by someone who has already died, by all means, do not make a saint out of this person or put a slab over it and pretend that nothing ever happened. To get over this hurt, you have to deal with the anger that this experience or experiences have caused in you. You need to talk to someone you trust about the thoughts and feelings that are welling up inside of you. You can even write a letter to the deceased person stating why you have a right to be angry. Then pay attention to any signs or messages that you may receive from the other side.

How Does Practicing the Art of Forgiveness Benefit Us?

1. Being resentful and angry raises our blood pressure, and long-term hypertension can wreak havoc on our health. All types of other stress-related illnesses may also begin to manifest in us if this situations goes on too long. We may be plagued with headaches,

stomachaches, all kinds of other aches and pains, insomnia, fatigue, autoimmune disorders, and just about any imaginable illness under the sun. Prolonged resentment and anger are toxic to your body; therefore, coming to terms with people and coming to that place of forgiveness will bring your body out of a state of "dis-ease," which leads to disease and back into a state of healthy balance.

2. **Study after study has shown that forgiveness is good for both our physical health and our mental health.** Ultimately, when we choose to forgive, we choose to live longer, healthier, and happier lives.

3. **Forgiveness allows us to leave the past behind and to begin to focus on the now.** Living in the moment allows us to embrace all that life still has to offer.

4. **We stop being the victim of those who have trespassed against us, and we take back our personal power.**

To Forgive or Not to Forgive?

1. If we don't forgive, we can find ourselves becoming obsessed about the past and lose sight of living in the now, which ultimately has disastrous effects on the future. When we truly forgive, we close the door on the past, and new doors to a happier future open up.

2. If we don't forgive properly, our bitterness begins to sour all of our relationships. Forgiving others allows us to open up again and to allow good people to come into our lives. All of our relationships stay healthy and evolve in positive and healing ways. We'll learn to trust our guts and know that we will have ample warning if and when others are not acting in our best interests.

3. Not forgiving can cause us to spiral downward psychologically into a state of depression, which really is anger turned inward and a feeling of hopelessness. Forgiveness rids us of angry feelings and opens us up to feelings of renewed hope.

Forgiving Those Who Have Trespassed against Us

Finally, when you have done everything humanly possible to forgive, but still resentment and revenge burn in your very soul, then you must turn over this experience and those feelings to God to be processed via the instrument of divine grace. Grace will allow the miracle of forgiveness to be processed for you, and one day this heavy cross will be off your back, and you will feel the freedom that true God-given forgiveness brings.

Questions for Self-Analysis

1. Is there someone you need to forgive? Can you begin taking the proper steps, as outlined in this chapter, to begin the forgiveness process? Write down the things that you need to do to start this process going.

2. Do you need to forgive yourself for some situation? Can you begin to take the necessary steps toward making amends for your actions? Is this a situation in which you were the offended party, and yet, you still haven't forgiven yourself for allowing this situation to happen? Write down the steps you need to take in order to forgive yourself.

Seven

Your Sixth So-Called Good Trait:
Your Need to Make Peace at Any Price
Or, I Shut the Hell Up and Don't Air My Dirty
Laundry

One-half the troubles of this life can be traced to saying yes too quickly and not saying no soon enough.

—Henry Wheeler Shaw

Finding True Peace on Earth

Peace I leave with you. My peace I give to you; not as the world gives, gives I to you. Don't let your heart be troubled, neither let it be fearful.

—John 14:27

What did Jesus mean when he spoke the above words? How would the true peace God offers be different from the peace the world offers? The answers to these two simple questions hold the key to your finding true and everlasting peace within yourself and ultimately within the world.

What the world offers us for the most part is peace at any price. It may cost us our health, our wealth, our life, and our sanity, but we, *The Great Enablers* of the world, try and try again to keep the peace, no matter what the personal cost to us may be. Once upon a time, to be a peacemaker was a high evolution for human beings. But *The Enlightened Ones* know that there is a time for peace and a time for war. This book will help you to know, in the very deepest part of your being, when and how to fight your battles. It will also help you achieve the ultimate outcome that you are hoping for: true, lasting peace; not the peace at any price that shutting up and allowing others to get away with murder brings. The "peace-at-any-price" philosophy comes with a high price tag and ultimately costs us our psychological and physical health.

Practice saying this heartfelt plea: "Dear Lord, I pray that you may teach me how to do what's best for everyone, including myself." This is the liberating and peace-bearing prayer that will lead you away from the "peace-at-any-price" mentality and toward the true peace of God.

As you daily say this prayer, your life will be guided by the powers that be, the good ones, that is. On this guided tour to true peace, please don't be surprised if, at first, this venture quakes the very earth you walk upon, rocking your boat and everyone else's boat as well. Sadly, at times, you may be left feeling crucified and alone. This will be your "Jesus moment." As you defy the masses, you'll be shocked to discover that even your so-called friends may not back you. It's excruciatingly painful to feel like an army of one, fighting a battle without any backup. However, in your darkest hour, you'll earn a miracle, and an army of angels will back you, giving you the strength you need to carry on.

The Peacemakers

The Great Enablers are, by nature, peacemakers who rarely express anger, even when people have hurt or betrayed them. They will, however, stand up for others, and they're fiercely protective of their own. This chapter will show you why and how you need to love yourself the way you love your own children or the way you love those nearest and dearest to you.

The Great Enablers have been conditioned to be the people-pleasers, the yes-men, and for this reason they tend to be taken advantage of. They're Christian martyrs, self-sacrificing to the point of sainthood, and the leaders of the "nice-guys-finish-last" crowd. If you're one of these kinds of people, you'll need to see the many reasons behind your need to please. Then you'll need to learn how to change this life-draining pattern of behavior.

Ultimately, people-pleasing keeps people stuck in the mind-set of victim consciousness. People who give too much are easy targets for *The Unfixables,* who just love to take advantage of others. It's only a matter of time before being used and abused by others leads the Peace-at-Any-Price People to be filled with resentment. After a while, they aren't angry at the people who take advantage of them; they're angry with themselves for allowing it. The first step to healing any negative behavior is becoming aware of it. Then you have to begin practicing behavior modification, which basically means learning new ways of behaving and being vigilant in enforcing them. From time to time you may fall off the wagon and find yourself back to your old habit of trying to make peace at any price, but when you catch yourself doing this, your awareness of this negative pattern will guide you back on the right path again.

When you're guilty of making peace at any price, you're not being part of the solution; rather, you're being part of the problem. Your fear of what **The Unfixables** of the world will do keeps you trapped in the magical thinking that if I just go along with things and don't rock the boat, nothing bad will happen to me. Yes, of course, we all know that **The Unfixables** play by their own rules, and they never play fair. Just know that when you learn how and when to stand up to **The Unfixables**, the world will become a much better place. Placating a monster doesn't make it go away; it just feeds the damn thing!

Keep in mind that saying yes when you really mean no is a habit, a bad one, and at times it's an addiction. People-pleasers are addicted to pleasing others. Pleasing others makes you feel needed, and sometimes it can make you even feel superior to others, more "Christ-like" or "Buddha-like" than others. All behaviors have some positive payoff for the players, and you might want to examine what positive payoffs you get out of playing the part of the "Holier-than-thou Martyr."

Eighteen Traits of People-Pleasers

1. People-pleasers would rather go down with the Titanic than rock the boat. The mere thought of stirring up muddy waters makes them sick to their stomachs, break out in hives, or hyperventilate so badly that they need to carry a brown bag with them, just in case some disagreement might ensue.

2. They can never say the words "enough is enough." They'd rather carry fifty crosses than put one down and catch the flack that might follow.

3. They avoid arguments and disagreements at all cost. They can feel their insides churning when a fight might be about to happen, and they placate everyone around them just to keep the peace.

4. They were, more often than not, bullied and abused by parents, siblings, and other family members when they were growing up. This instilled in them from early on a high tolerance for abuse. This high tolerance for pain allows them to suck it up and not react in ways that would inspire further chaos, violence, or aggression enacted upon them.

5. They make a lot of excuses for abuse; therefore, they feel they must accept whatever crap is dumped on them, believing other people have valid reasons for behaving the way that they do. Ironically, although people-pleasers themselves have usually been abused as children, they don't think that gives them a license to abuse others, and they honestly try to be better people because of what was done to them.

6. They're really great at stuffing down their feelings. They tend to plaster on a smile in the morning, and come hell or high water, that smile never budges.

7. They tend to put other people's needs and desires before their own. They are plagued with unbearable guilt when they put themselves first, or when they speak up for themselves, and they will do almost anything to avoid this anxiety-producing emotion.

8. They don't like to make decisions and just wait to see what others want before saying anything.

9. If they were raised by a tyrannical, irrational, rage-aholic parent or guardian, the beatings and verbal abuse may have been so great when they spoke up that they learned to be submissive in order to avoid the nuclear explosion speaking up elicited.

10. People-pleasers live in dread of the fallout that might occur should they say no. So they just say yes to everything.

11. They live in a constant state of fight or flight. Because fighting is so frightening to them, they tend to go into a flight mode via avoiding the situation, removing themselves from it, or by fleeing in their minds from the situation by denying, suppressing, or repressing the entire scenario.

12. For the most part they're pushovers and just do what they're told to.

13. People-pleasers need the approval of others. They fear others might find them selfish or lazy if they say no. They can't stand when people don't like them, which, by the way, is a form of narcissism. If you're a people-pleaser, meditate on that one!

14. They have massive fears of being abandoned, ostracized, judged, ridiculed, or exiled by others, and these overwhelming fears keep them trapped to their peacemaker roles.

15. People-pleasers have trouble setting healthy boundaries. They haven't learned when too much is too much or when enough is enough! People-pleasers allow others to rape their boundaries and take advantage of them. Learning to set healthy boundaries can be as simple as stating the times when people can call you, how many hours you are available for work or to help, and what others can and cannot expect of you.

16. People-pleasers have a need to please everyone. They seek to make everyone happy and to be everything to everyone. This is an unrealistic and unhealthy mind-set. There are only so many hours in a day, and learning to manage that time is the key to a happy and healthy life.

17. Perhaps the worst part of being a people-pleaser is dealing with the people that this kind of behavior attracts: *The Unfixables*.

18. People-pleasers somehow believe that everything is all their fault, and for that reason, it's their job to fix everyone and everything. Again, this is a form of narcissism to believe that everything that happens in the world happens because of you. If you want to stop being a people-pleaser, then stop thinking that you're God. All the pain, suffering, and misery in the world didn't begin the day you were born, nor will it end the day you die.

If you truly wish to make the world a better place, then you'll have to learn to speak up and to punish those people who need punishing, and in order to do so, you just might have to rock a few boats. So be it!

⸨⸨⸨

Remember: What we don't want to talk about, the old "pink elephant in the room," is exactly what you must talk about. Stop dancing around the obvious.

⸨⸨⸨

How and When to Just Say No!

Every time you say yes when you mean no, you give away your power.

The art of learning to say no is truly mastering this simple truth: **Say what you mean, and mean what you say, without being mean about it.**

Let's take some time to analyse the above three-part statement. What does it mean to say what you mean? If you don't want to do something, then this means saying so. It doesn't mean saying yes, then regretting that answer later on. If you really don't want to do something or go somewhere, then say so.

For instance, your friend wants to go see a play that you really have no interest in seeing. Usually you just agree to go, lay out a lot of money you'd rather use for something else, schlep to the city, and sleep through the show, inwardly cursing yourself out for being such a wimp and allowing yourself to be suckered into going where you didn't want to go in the first place. How could you handle this situation differently, without offending your friend and still taking your own feelings into account? You could simply, firmly, and kindly say, "No, thank you. I really don't want to see that play because I'm not a fan of that playwright. But I'm sure that you can find someone else to go with you who would really love that experience."

The second part of the sentence, "mean what you say," lets you know that you have the right to express your opinion. You're going to have to learn to speak up despite your fears. In any given situation, be realistic in evaluating where your fear is coming from. Ruminate on whether this fear is a rational fear, or is it just your long-term conditioning to people please. If you realize that your fear is mainly in your own mind and that no real harm will come to you if you state your case, then speaking up is definitely the right thing to do.

The third part of the sentence, "without being mean about it," is the key to everything. Just say the words firmly and politely. If you've bottled up your feelings for weeks, months, and years at a time, when you finally do let them out, you'll probably sound like a raving lunatic. You need to speak up often and on a regular basis so that this "saying what you mean without being mean about it" becomes second nature.

People-Pleasing: The Magnet That Draws
Louses, Lowlifes, and Liars to You

The Unfixables gravitate to people-pleasers. The people-pleasers' need to help others, combined with their easygoing temperaments and bad self-esteem issues, all add up in *The Unfixables'* book to mean easy prey.

If you're a people-pleaser, come to realize that *The Unfixables* instinctively know that you'll go along with whatever they want. They know that you don't like confrontation, and you'll stuff down your own needs and thoughts and go with their flow. In small doses, you can take anything, but a daily diet of this kind of nonsense will leave you feeling depressed. As we've previously discussed, depression is anger turned inward and a feeling of helplessness. When you're dealing with *The Self-Serving Narcissists* of the world, you'll always feel like you're stuffing down anger. At times, you'll be angry at them, but mostly you'll be angry at yourself for putting up with so much crap. As for the feelings of helplessness that accompany depression, well, that just goes with the territory, if you're going to keep on trying to please *The Unfixables,* who are insatiable Energy Vampires.

Because of their high tolerance for pain, Peace-at-Any-Price People often attract mean-spirited, violent, self-centered people into their world. People-pleasers make a lot of excuses for abuse, discounting, denying, or ignoring a lot of sins committed against them by *The Unfixables.* People-pleasers feel sorry for everyone, and that compassion is further taken advantage of.

Once you stand up to *The Unfixables*, they'll try to manipulate you to going back to being your old blindfolded, submissive self. They have several strategies that have proven effective in the past, and they will resort to one or many of these, hoping to keep the insurrection down. They'll start by "yes-ing" you to death. They'll tell you everything you want to hear, even admitting a little bit of truth. They might try to deny any wrongdoing. If that doesn't work, they know that people-pleasers always think everything is all their fault, and *The Unfixables* will turn the tables and twist and turn the truth so much, you won't know which way is up, and you'll once again give them the benefit of the doubt. They might try bullying you. They'll threaten to abandon you, punish you, or ruin you if you don't go back to acting like you used to. They will guilt you, blame you, shame you, and maim you, if that's what it takes to break you.

During these trying times, when you're in the midst of one of these ace manipulators, I want you to love yourself the way you love your own children, or would love your own children. If you would tell your beloved child to turn the other cheek, then for you to do so in this particular instance would more than likely be the right response. If you'd tell your child to sue the bastard or walk away, then that's the proper response. Coming to the place of self-love is paramount for people-pleasers, because that's been beaten out of them. Once you come from the place of self-love, you can see clear to your intentions. Your intention in punishing or leaving this person is not to hurt anyone, but to teach him or her a much-needed lesson. This kind of reaction is coming from a place of self-love and self-preservation.

Dissecting Your Past to Find the Root of Your People-Pleasing

Those of us raised in a war zone, where one or both of our parents could have and should have been referred to as *mein führer*, learned to live in fear of the angry outbursts and irrational rage that these people could launch our way.

If you spent your childhood walking on eggshells in an effort to dodge parental, rage-filled wrath, this avoidance behavior planted the seeds for you to become a people-pleaser. Later on in life, when you encountered other *Self-serving Narcissists* in your private life or work life, you applied the same kind of avoidance strategy in dealing with them. This translated into staying out of their way, placating them, and giving in to them. The fear of what *The Unfixables* might do to you always weighs heavily in your heart and mind.

From this day forward, you're going to have to learn to live in the now. You're a grown-up and not a child anymore. Remember that as a child you most certainly were a victim of abusive adults; but now you're an adult, and adults can't be victims. Once you come to see that your extreme fear of angering others stems from your dysfunctional childhood, and that for the most part it's an over-the-top fear, you'll learn to live in the here and now and address each person and each situation appropriately. True, your crazy boss may fire you for speaking up—which could be a blessing in disguise—but he or she probably won't start beating you up or aiming a gun at your head. Once you stop fearing *The Unfixables,* they usually move on to find easier prey. It may take a while for these parasites to let go of you, but that's where drawing healthy boundaries, standing your ground, and punishing these people for their behaviors goes a long way in freeing you from their destructive ways.

If your childhood was overwrought with fear of a parental figure, you need to start looking deep inside yourself to forgive that person, but not the unforgivable actions that were committed against you. Coming to terms with the physical, psychological, verbal, emotional, or sexual abuse that you suffered at the hands of this parent is one thing. But your real anger goes much deeper, and this anger could rightfully be aimed at the better parent. As adults, we can forgive the crazy parent; after all, they were nuts. It's our need to protect the image of the better parent that really needs addressing. Sadly, it's usually the people-pleasers, *The Good-to-a-Fault People* and *The Great Enablers,* who didn't protect their children enough from *The Unfixables* and from *The Dr. Jekyll/Mr. Hyde-types.* By their very natures, *The Great Enablers* make a lot of excuses for abuse, but all of us have to deal with the reality that it isn't OK that people hurt us or that others allowed it to happen.

Setting Healthy Boundaries

Just as good fences make for good neighbors, healthy boundaries make for healthy relationships. By setting and keep healthy boundaries, we define the kinds of relationship we want with others. Our words and actions are the building blocks we use to construct healthy boundaries.

Since *The Unfixables* of the world think that they have a right to rape boundaries, it's up to the rest of the world to set them straight by setting and maintaining healthy boundaries. It's up to you to draw a line in the sand, and to stick to it no matter how much guilt, shame, blame, or rage the other person throws your way. It's your job to stand your ground and not back down, cave in, or give in, and you can only do this when you're no longer afraid to assert yourself, regardless of the consequences. You're the gatekeeper. No one can gain access to your world, inner or outer, without your permission.

Boundary issues are power struggles. *The Unfixables* love to take on the role of the master over us, and they love to watch us jump through hoops to please them. People-pleasers take on the role of slave. They're *The Donkey People*, doing the work of eight people, and *The Self-Serving Narcissists* can smell them a block away. If you're one of *The Donkey People*, then it's up to you to learn to say, "Enough is enough." It's up to you to put down everyone's cross but your own.

Since the advent of the cell phone, people seem to think that they have the right to call or text others all day long, to the point that we're all feeling like we're victims of textual abuse. I have an expression that I use when a family member, client, or friend keeps calling me about every little problem they're encountering all day long: "What would you do if I were dead? Then go do it!" People can only take advantage of you and walk all over you if *you* allow it. Let people know when you're available to speak, and don't be afraid to tell them when you would like some time for yourself!

The Unfixables think that they can bother us 24-7. They truly believe that we should drop whatever we're doing at their beck and call and bail them out, help them, fix something or other, or be there as their sounding board. If you have a person or a lot of people like that in your life, then you need to let them know when and how they can reach you. These Energy Vampires will suck you dry if you let them.

The Self-Serving Narcissists are great at pushing your guilt buttons, and you're just going to have to learn to be equally adept at shutting the guilt button off in your own head. It's not your job to fix everything, rescue everyone, or save the world. It's your job to try and fix yourself, rescue yourself, and save yourself. In doing so, you will heal your issues and become a beacon of light for the world to see.

If you're the "go-to" person that everyone seems to turn to whenever something needs doing, then it's up to you to clearly pick and choose those times that you want to help, or that you can help. You also need to find the courage to say no when you really can't help, or truly don't want to do something, even if you conceivably could do it.

Five Steps to Stop Saying Yes When You Really Mean No!

1. Do not immediately answer a request to take on a project or to commit to doing something.

2. Tell the person you need to think about it first, and that you need to check your schedule.

3. If after careful thought and consideration, the answer is "No, I can't do this," then tell the person so.

4. Do not allow for wiggle room. Just say "no," mean it, and that's your story and you're sticking to it!

5. Remember: you don't have to give a litany of reasons why you can't do something. Simply say, "After careful consideration, I've come to realize that I can't take on another project right now." End of story.

Gina, *The Great Enabler*, and Vinnie, *The Unfixable*

In this case study, Gina's Great Enabler traits will be put in parenthesis and italicized, and Vinnie's Unfixable traits will be put in parenthesis and bolded.

The first thing you'd notice about Gina, a forty-year-old woman, is her childlike innocence and spontaneous nature. Gina hugs everyone she sees and lights up every room just by entering it. She brings out the best in everyone, and she loves to see the good in everyone. *(Seeing the world through rose-colored glasses)* Gina is a multitalented entertainer who can wow you with her vocals, her dancing, and her guitar playing.

The first thing that you'd notice about her forty-five-year-old, soon-to-be ex- husband, Vinnie, is his boyish good looks and aloof manner. You might also notice that he never seems to answer the question that you're asking him, and that he'll switch the topic to talk about what he wants to talk about, and only what he wants to talk about. **(Manipulation: lies of omission and narcissism, since everything always has to be about Vinnie)**

Gina knew Vinnie most of her life. Their parents grew up together in the same neighborhood in Brooklyn, and migrated out to the suburbs together, buying matching, side-by-side houses on the south shore of Long Island. Gina called Vinnie's parents Aunt and Uncle, and Vinnie called her parents Aunt and Uncle, and it wasn't until Gina was ten that she discovered that she and Vinnie weren't blood relatives.

From the get-go, Gina adored Vinnie. No, Gina worshipped Vinnie. *(Seeing the world through rose-colored glasses)* Because of their five-year age difference, Gina didn't really get to see all that much of Vinnie during his teen years, since Vinnie hung out with his friends on the other side of town. Still, at the family get-togethers, Gina would always try to get Vinnie to talk with her, or play ball, board games, or cards with her. A lot of times he just ignored her or blew her off, and on more than one occasion he called her names, bullied her, and once even threatened to beat her up if she didn't scram. **("The Dictator" manipulator)** Gina always forgave him, saying, "He was just tired or he doesn't feel good." *(Forgiving too easily and too often, and making excuses for abuse)*

When she was thirteen and he was eighteen, Gina thought that Vinnie was the smartest, funniest, handsomest guy in the world. To her, it seemed like he could do nothing wrong and everything right. *(Seeing the world through rose-colored glasses)* When he wasn't riding his motorcycle, he would be fiddling around his house or her house, fixing anything that was broken. On numerous occasions, Gina remember overhearing her father say, "I can't stand doing anything with Vinnie, because we always have to do everything his way, because he thinks he knows everything!" **("It's My Way or No Way" manipulator and "I am Smarter and More Gifted Than Anyone Else" and the "Stupidvisor" manipulator)** To Gina, whether Vinnie was riding a motorcycle or driving a car or a big delivery truck, he looked like a knight in shining armor. *(Seeing the world through rose-colored glasses)*

All throughout Vinnie's teen years, Gina made herself block out the images of him with his string of girlfriends, always skinny blonde-types. Once she heard his mother shout over the fence to her mother, "Vinnie will never settle down. He's a real ladies' man like his grandfather!" *(Practicing the art of denial to keep the rose-colored glasses on)*

When Gina was fifteen, she heard the two families whispering a lot about Vinnie. But whenever Gina asked what they were talking about, they told her to go to her room and to mind her own business. Gina kept her ears glued to walls and eventually found out that Vinnie had been arrested for driving the getaway car used in a gas station robbery. She refused to believe that Vinnie would do anything like that, but her father said, "He got caught red-handed." *(Rose-colored glasses combined with being loyal to a fault)*

Gina wouldn't see Vinnie again until her high school graduation party. When he walked into the party, Gina almost stopped breathing; she thought Vinnie looked more handsome than ever. The first thing he said to her that night was, "Has it really been that long since I last saw you? I can't believe that you're all grown up!" They spent the whole evening together talking about the good old days. When Gina finally mustered up the nerve to ask him about the robbery, at first Vinnie tried to change the topic. When Gina brought it up a second time, he said, "I took the rap for a buddy of mine. That's the kind of good guy I am!" **(Manipulation: Not taking responsibility for his actions and making himself come out smelling like roses)** Gina believed him. *(Seeing the world through rose-colored glasses)*

After that night, it would be another five years before they would talk again, and this would be at the wedding of some mutual family friends. Gina told Vinnie that she'd been engaged the year before, but her fiancé had broken off the engagement a few months back, saying that he wasn't going to play second fiddle to her acting career. He told her, "It's me or the theater, but you can't have both." Gina was a rising star at this point and landed one part after another in regional and off Broadway plays. She was devastated that he would ask her to choose between the two things she loved most in the world—him and the stage.

When Gina told Vinnie that she'd just received a call from her ex the other day and that he wanted to get back together with her, Vinnie told her, "The guy's a loser. How could he ask you to give up your career?" Basically, Vinnie spent the whole night convincing Gina to remain single and look for someone who would be supportive of her career. **(Manipulation: Telling her what she wanted to hear to convince her that he thought just like her!)** People couldn't help noticing how much time they were spending together at the wedding, and even commented on how well they looked together when they were dancing. Gina had hoped to see Vinnie again, but nothing seemed to come of that night.

A few months later, Vinnie got into a really bad truck accident. The second Gina learned of this, she rushed to the hospital to be by his side. When he was released from the hospital, Gina spent all of her spare time taking care of him, even turning down the coveted role of Maria in a regional revival of *West Side Story*. After that, they "fell into a relationship," as Gina describes it. They had the most passionate times in bed, and Vinnie could never seem to get enough of her. Sometimes it bothered her that he never used the words "*boyfriend*" or "*girlfriend*," but she told herself that this didn't matter, since they were inseparable. A few months later, he asked her to move into his apartment.

Within a few days of moving in with him, Gina noticed that Vinnie had a very short fuse. Gina always tried to placate him at these times. (*A need to make peace at any price, people-pleasing*) Gina soon learned that there was no avoiding Vinnie's temper tantrums because the slightest thing could set him off. (**"The Rage-Aholic" manipulator**) After every tirade, he would say that he was sorry, but that didn't stop him from doing the same thing over and over again. (**Manipulation: Pretending that he was sorry to get himself off the hook**) Gina always forgave him, justifying his behaviors one way or another. *(Forgiving too easily and too often, and making excuses for abuse)* Other times, he appeared to be really out of it, and he would say, "I'm just tired. You're always nagging me and it's wearing me down." (**Manipulation: Guilting her to believe that she was the cause of his moodiness and fatigue, and turning the tables on her**)

One night, Vinnie's mother said, "Vinnie's taking an awful lot of pain pills." She suggested, "He'd better get off of those things." When Gina told Vinnie what his mother had said to her about his drug use, he went ballistic. He started cursing at her, and telling her that everyone was against him, and how mad he was at her for siding with his meddling mother. He also screamed, "How can I get off the pain pills when you keep being such a big pain in my ass!" (**Manipulation: having a temper tantrum and bullying her to scare her silent, and guilting her about turning on him and blaming her for being the reason that he can't heal**) Gina felt terrible about the whole incident and apologized profusely to him. She felt that if she were more patient and loving, Vinnie wouldn't need to take so many pain pills. No matter what he did, Gina swore that she would remain calm and supportive of him. *(It's all my fault, and it's my job to fix everything and everybody, and keeping the peace at any price)* From that day forward, no matter what Vinnie did, she would never again confide or talk to anyone about Vinnie's behavior. *(Loyal to a fault)*

A year later, Vinnie, recovered from his injuries and went back to work. At this point, Gina tried to get her neglected acting career on track again. It wasn't easy. She took a day job as a waitress in the meantime, and she was thrilled to death when she got a call back from an audition she had gone on a few weeks before. "Vinnie!" She jumped up, screaming. "I got the job. I got the job doing summer stock in Connecticut!" Vinnie said, "That's great, but if you take it, don't think I'll be here waiting around for you." **(Manipulation: threatening her with the loss of love)** Gina was stunned. History was repeating itself. Hadn't Vinnie been the one to tell her to give up on her ex if he weren't supportive of her career? **(Manipulation: telling her what she wanted to hear)**

Gina spent several sleepless nights wondering what she should do. She couldn't bear the thought of losing Vinnie and cried without end after she turned down the offer. All that summer she kept waiting on tables and waiting for something else in the theater to manifest. Meanwhile, Vinnie's mood swings got worse and worse, and Gina walked on eggshells most of the time, not wanting to set him off. *(A need to make peace at any price)*

During this time, Gina found a stash of pills in Vinnie's desk drawer and asked him where he got them. He told her they were the pills left from his accident. He also threw a hissy fit. "Stop spying on me and treating me like a bad little boy!" he screamed. "You're worse than my mother ever was." **(Manipulation: name calling, bullying, and turning the tables to make it look as if she were the one in the wrong)** Gina wanted to believe him, and she didn't want to fight with him. *(Seeing the good in others, and giving them the benefit of the doubt, combined with keeping the peace at any price)* It wasn't easy, but she tried hard to ignore her gut feeling that he was lying. *(Not trusting your inner guidance)*

No matter how much money Gina made working overtime, Vinnie always complained that they were in debt. He blamed her for spending too much money, even though Gina never spent any money on herself, just on household expenses. **(Manipulation: making her believe they were in debt because of her spending habits)**

After three years of waiting on tables, Gina decided to go back to school to finish her teaching degree. Between waiting on tables and going back to school, Gina barely got to see Vinnie. One day, while studying for her finals, she got a call from Vinnie's mother, who said, "Gina, I know you're busy bettering yourself, but I don't know how you can just ignore the fact that Vinnie is stoned day and night." Gina was stunned. "What?" she said. His mother started screaming, "He's all drugged up and you don't know about it? Everybody knows about it. He needs to go into rehab, and I hope you'll support his family's decision on this one. By the way, you do know that he's been out of work for two months, don't you?" Gina couldn't believe that she'd been so blind. *(Seeing the world through rose-colored glasses)* Suddenly things started making sense. That's why there was never any money. That was why he was always so moody. When Gina confronted him on this, he said, "What do you want me to do all night, when you're never here?" **(Manipulation: Guilting her that his drug use was her fault and not taking responsibility for his own actions)** He then began shouting, "It's always about you, you, you and your hotshot career and your need to be better than everybody else." **(Manipulation: Bullying, shaming, blaming, and turning the tables on her to make her believe that she was being the narcissistic and selfish one)**

Gina told herself that it was the drugs talking. *(Seeing the world through rose-colored glasses and making excuses for abuse)* Vinnie went to rehab, and Gina began looking over the bills. She almost had a breakdown when she realized how in debt they really were. She also noticed that he had taken out several credit cards in her name, and that each one of these was maxed out. Her first reaction was to be furious with him for forging her name and not telling her about the credit cards. She called up her parents. "How could he do this?" she cried. Her father was furious. He said, "If he drops dead from all his drugs, you'll still be left here to pay off his debts. I want you to call up the credit card companies and tell them what he did." Gina began crying. "Daddy, I can't do that. He was on drugs. He didn't know what he was doing." *(Inability to love yourself the way you would love your own children, making excuses for abuse, and an inability to punish the inner circle)* Gina was determined to just pay off this debt, so Vinnie would have one less thing to worry about. *(Her belief that she was her brother's keeper and her need to fix everything and everyone)*

Still, she couldn't sleep for weeks and could barely function at work or at school, wondering how they were ever going to get out of the financial hole they were in. She was plagued with guilt feelings that if she had been paying more attention to Vinnie, all of this mess might never have happened. *(It's all my fault, well-meaning narcissistic thinking)*

A few months later, she finished school and got a teaching job. Vinnie finished with rehab, got another job, and appeared to be heading in the right direction.

Although teaching wasn't what she really wanted to do, she tried to tell herself that she was happy and that she had a lot to be grateful for. To her surprise, because of her musical background, she was given the opportunity to direct the school musical. Gina loved doing this, but Vinnie complained constantly about how she was never home in the evenings and how once again he came last. **(Manipulation: Guilting her and making her feel that she was being selfish)** Gina tried her best to give Vinnie as much attention as she could, but he would sulk and complain all the same. He told her, "I sacrificed a lot to help you go back to school, and now this is how you reward me?" **(Manipulation: "After all I did for you—The Guilt Tripper" Manipulator)** Gina told him that he needed a hobby. She suggested that he join a gym.

Pretty soon, it appeared that Vinnie was hooked on the gym, going every night for several hours after work. Even when school was out for the summer and Gina was only working a few hours a day at a local acting school, Vinnie would spend every night at the gym. Gina found herself feeling lonely, but when she confronted Vinnie, he said, "Welcome to my world." **(Manipulation: turning the tables on her)** It was only when Gina threatened to move out that Vinnie started to spend more time with her. He also asked her to marry him, and Gina spent the rest of that year working and preparing for their wedding. Her gut told her something wasn't kosher. *(Not trusting your gut)* When she told Vinnie that she felt that something was wrong between them, he told her, "You're just like your mother—paranoid." **(Manipulation: Denying the truth of what she was saying and making her feel that she was doing something wrong, name calling)**

Even though she sensed that Vinnie was being distant and that he didn't give a damn about the wedding, Gina tried to tell herself that things would get better once they were married and the stress of planning the wedding was over. *(Giving him the benefit of the doubt)* It wasn't just Gina who noticed Vinnie's indifference to their upcoming nuptials. The night before the wedding, Gina's father asked her, "Are you sure you want to do this?"

The wedding went on as planned, but things only got worse after they tied the knot. Vinnie was rarely home in the evenings, and whenever she asked him about his whereabouts, he would just say, "I like to go to the gym." Gina suggested that perhaps she could join the gym so that they could spend some time together, and Vinnie started screaming, "Can't a guy have a space of his own?" **(Manipulation: bullying and shaming her)**

One day, Gina noticed that Vinnie looked stoned. When she asked him about this, he stomped out of the house. **(Manipulation: Making her feel that she had done something wrong; lying by omission by not answering the question)** For about two hours Gina set on the couch crying. Then she put on her coat, got in her car, and headed over to the gym. She told me, "It was as if I were possessed that night." Just as she drove up to the gym, she saw a blonde woman, about twenty, getting into Vinnie's car. She watched them kiss. She jumped out of her car and started banging on his windshield. Vinnie and the woman stopped kissing. He got out of the car and said, "How dare you come to the gym!" (**Manipulation: Once again, Vinnie turns the tables on Gina**)

Gina, stunned, got back in her car. She was crying hysterically as she drove down the block. She went through a red light and crashed into another car. Vinnie, with the blonde woman still in the front seat, drove down to the accident scene. He yelled at Gina, who was in excruciating pain from the accident, "The drama queen! You always have to be the drama queen, don't you?" (**Manipulation: Name calling and turning the tables to make Gina feel she was in the wrong, and not taking responsibility for his infidelity**)

Gina later found out that Vinnie had been seeing the blonde woman, who turned out to be a personal trainer in the gym, for more than a year. Gina is now in the final stages of divorce from Vinnie. She is learning to stop kicking herself in the head for not seeing the writing on the wall sooner, and for being too good and loyal to a fault. She's working hard to keep the rose-colored glasses off and to forgive herself for not trusting her own gut instincts. She's also learning to speak up and to stop making peace at any price.

Messages from the other side: Throughout the sessions that I conducted with Gina, she was guided by her Aunt Maryann who had recently died of uterine cancer. Aunt Maryann came through saying, "Vinnie is too much like my husband, Vito, for my liking."

Gina told me that everyone knew that Vito had cheated on Maryann from day one. It was part of the family gossip, and Gina was shocked the first time Maryann compared Vinnie to Vito. In fact, Gina thought that I must have been hearing something wrong. I insisted that Maryann was a very loud and clear voice. I also told her that Maryann would pop a thought in her head to let her know when she could check up on Vinnie and find out what he was really up to. Looking back, Gina told me that it had to have been Aunt Maryann guiding her to go to the gym at the exact moment when she would catch Vinnie kissing his girlfriend.

Gina told me that she is very grateful for the guidance her aunt gave her from the grave, and that it's her aunt who continues to give her the strength to move on.

Questions for Self-Analysis

1. When you were growing up, was there a parental figure who scared you into silence?

2. Can you remember an incident from your childhood when this person intimidated you so much that you bit your tongue and did what you were told to do, even though you knew that it was wrong to do so?

3. Which people in your life intimidate you now?

4. Have you ever rewarded intimidating behavior by giving in, shutting up, or tolerating a tirade just to keep the peace?

5. Have you been enabling someone's behavior because you're afraid of the confrontation that will occur should you speak your mind?

Eight

Summing It All Up
Or, So You Think You're Going to Screw Me Again?
Think Twice: For Once in My Life I've Got My
Head Screwed On Right

When you've got your head screwed on right, no one can screw with you. Just think about how liberating it's going to be to state, "*Hey, you can't screw me anymore, because I've stopped screwing with my own head.*"

Over the course of the next few weeks, I want you to reexamine all of your past relationships with family members, lovers, coworkers, and employers, or any relationship in which you tolerated abuse for any length of time. Why did you stick around for so long, even when your gut told you to leave? Why did you spend years at a bad job or in a bad marriage while you kept tossing and turning in your head the pros and cons of staying or moving on? Why did you live in a prolonged state of limbo, asking yourself every day, "*Should I stay or should I go?*" At the end of the day, you have to take responsibility for the fact that you've stayed far too long in bad relationships because of your own insecurities and fears.

There's no one on this planet who's so totally unselfish that he or she would stay for any length of time in a toxic relationship if there weren't some payoff in that particular situation. Toxic relationships serve many purposes. Unless you understand the karmic lessons that you were supposed to learn from toxic relationships and fully understand the payoff that you were receiving in staying put, then you'll just keep finding yourself stuck, time and time again, in no-win situations.

Some of the Reasons, Purposes, and Payoffs for Staying in Bad Relationships

1) Unhealed childhood issues—If you haven't dealt with your own pain and abuse from the past, your own repressed, suppressed, and denied anger will need to surface some way, somehow, somewhere. Now, if you're one of *The Great Enablers*, who stuff down all their anger issues, you can bet your bottom dollar that having a love affair with one of *The Unfixables* will give you plenty of opportunities to get angry; therefore, you can feel justified in raging, screaming, and hitting this person over the head with a frying pan. You can rationalize away your rage by saying that anyone can see he or she deserves it. This way, a nice person like you gets to rage behind closed doors, venting some of your pent-up anger, and then you can go out into the world and look normal. Eventually, *The Good-to-a-Fault People* get out of these toxic relationships because they don't like the person they've become. They learn to move beyond their anger, and even if their partners do deserve a good, quick kick in the ass, good people don't like being the ones to have to keep doing this. With that said, you're going to have to deal with your own anger and rage issues, or else every relationship that you're in will eventually turn toxic.

Toxic relationships do serve a legitimate purpose: they give people an opportunity to rage behind closed doors with people they supposedly love. If it weren't for toxic love affairs, there probably would be a lot more rabid people going up on rooftops with guns and blowing away innocent bystanders. For the most part, couples venting their pent-up anger from the past don't take their battles outside the home, where they could be a danger to society. The truth of the matter is this: It takes two **Self-serving Narcissists** (two of **The Unfixables**) to stay in a long-term toxic love affair. They both feel that the other partner is wrong; therefore, any anger they possess is justified.

2) Staying with the Devil You Know—Humans by nature fear change. **The Great Enablers** aren't usually great risk takers. They're calculated risk takers and have to mull over the consequences of leaving a job or leaving a relationship for a considerable amount of time. Even after all is said and done, they'll still flounder around in limbo for a long time before they make a move. Just know that it's always better to leave on your own accord and not wait around until the universe makes you leave. God is patient, but eventually, the rug will be pulled out from under you. Believe me; it hurts a lot more when the universe pulls the plug for you, or when the universe gives you a good, swift kick in the butt to move you forward!

Use this as a rule of thumb: if for more than one year, in any given situation, you've been unsure whether you should stay or you should go, it's time to leave, or at least take a time out, or a leave of absence, or to try a trial separation to see how you feel without this person, job, or situation. When we're doing the work that we're meant to do, living the lives we're born to lead, and in good relationships, our biggest fear is that these wonderful people or these precious things might be taken from us. We're certainly not sitting around wondering if we want them.

If you're feeling stuck in a place or in a relationship, but can't seem to find the door out, you're going to have to examine what fears might be keeping you there. Keep reading this book and asking the universe for guidance, and the answers will be revealed to you. Learn to turn your life over to a higher power and watch miracles begin to happen.

Most of us have some level of obsessive-compulsive disorder. OCD, with all its constant worry and guilt thoughts, can really keep us wavering back and forth and paralyzed by fear and anxiety. People with OCD spend a great deal of time *what-iffing this* and *what-iffing that*. They also do a great deal of Monday-morning quarterbacking: *If only I did this* or *if only I did that*. All this *what if this happens* and *what if that happens* and *if only this happened* or *if only that happened* has us living in the nebulous future, fearing the worst-case scenario, or staying stuck in the unchangeable past. This kind of circular thinking keeps people stuck in "the devil they know mind-set," because the impending doom this negative thinking portends can be truly terrifying. How many times have you heard yourself say, "What if I leave this relationship and I end up alone for the rest of my life?" Or, "What if things are worse after I leave?" Maybe you find yourself saying things, such as: "If only I were younger." "If only I did this sooner."

Stop with all the past regrets and worst-case future scenarios. All you know is that today stinks and something has to give. We all need to live in the moment. It's all we really know. If you're miserable in your present relationship and with your current life situation, then learn to practice the Law of Attraction. Visualize the many splendid things the future holds. Stop dwelling on past mistakes, and stop conjuring up imaginary future worst-case scenarios. Practice behavior modification; allow yourself no more than five minutes a day of *what-iffing* and *if only* thinking, then get up and deal with today's reality.

3) Financial fears—When it comes to jobs, careers, business partnerships, and marriages, money factors big-time in our decisions to terminate any of these relationships. Just remember that God would never ask you to sell your soul for money, since to do so would be an enactment of the prostitute archetype. You have to stop thinking that you can't make it in this world without these people, or this person, or this job. Believe in yourself and in your worth!

4) Women's collective unconscious fear that any man is better than no man—Historically, women really were dependent on men for their survival. Most women didn't work, and even if they wanted to, it certainly wasn't encouraged. There's no denying that times have changed, but human consciousness is slow to catch up, and each and every one of us has to work hard to erase the collective brainwashing that has been instilled in us since the dawn of time.

Most women still can't seem to leave a man even if they truly can survive financially on their own. It's the old acting out of women as chattel, going from being the property of their fathers to the property of a man. Before most women will leave a man, there must be another one on the horizon. The truth is that you aren't leaving one man for another; you're really leaving the first man because you have to. Eventually, this going from man to man will lead a woman to know that no knight in shining armor is going to rescue her. The man who comes to help us out of one relationship usually has clay feet, and is more like the past men than we care to know. In due time, this will be revealed. Walking away from a bad relationship and standing on your own two feet—and this holds for men as well—is the first step toward having a healthy relationship in the future.

5) Your fear of the unknown—Yes, it can seem scary to get out there in the larger world and get back in the dating game, or to go out job hunting, or to simply strike out on your own. This is your call to courage. Everyone has fear, but courage gives you the strength to go outside of your comfort zone to seek true fulfillment and happiness.

6) We always have to relive our parents' marriage— Somewhere along the line, we all have to relive our parents' marriage, mostly the marriage we saw before the age of five. During those early formative years, our minds were like sponges soaking up everything we heard and saw. Reliving your parents' marriage can be good news, if your parents had a happy, healthy, and loving relationship. On the flip side, if your parents' marriage was a train wreck, this can be very bad news.

Even the village idiot can figure out why we'd want to duplicate our parents' marriage if it had been a good one. It can be a little harder to figure out why in the world we'd want to duplicate a bad one. If we accept the premise that we're here on earth school to learn, evolve, and grow, the reasons are not all that complicated after all.

When we're young children, we tend to be very judgmental. We watch our parents' bickering and think, "If I were married, I'd never speak to my husband that way." Or, "If I had a wife, I'd never treat her like that." The universe registers those early-on thoughts, and when we grow up, it throws them back in our faces saying, "OK, you little know-it-all, let me see you do better."

Of course, when we're young, we have no idea how difficult it is to scratch a living out of the earth or how stressful life can be for grown-ups, even under the best of circumstances. So, we sat in judgment of our parents, all the while lacking the wisdom and knowledge we needed to see the situation from a more compassionate viewpoint. Only later on, after we find ourselves doing the same destructive song and dance that our parents did—and shockingly—sometimes doing even worse, do we begin to realize just how difficult love and life can be.

What lessons do you think the universe is trying to teach us via this painful experience? Basically, we're asked to stop being judgmental of others and to forgive our parents, for they knew not what they did.

If you're to move away from these destructive relationship patterns, you must first forgive your parents. Have you forgiven your parents for the sin of being all too human? Until you forgive them, you'll be doomed to repeat their marriage over and over again. This may well be the reason why your relationships always seem to start out great and then end in disaster. You're also asked to stop judging them. Yes, you can judge their actions as being unhealthy, destructive, or dysfunctional, but you're asked to stop judging them *personally*. Unless we stop judging our parents, we will surely become them.

Picture the three-year-old in you walking around thinking, "If I were married, no one would fight, or drink, or cheat because I'd be so lovey-dovey that I'd fix everyone and everything." Then you get a little bit older and you wonder, "Why the hell did they marry each other in the first place? Then you figure out that one or both of your parents were the Prince or Princess That Became the Beast. After that, you set out to prove that you could have fixed that beastly parent. So off you go and pick someone ten times worse than your worst parent, trying to prove that you could fix the Beast. I hope that after reading this book thus far, you've learned there's no fixing the Beast, aka *The Unfixables!*

Take some time to begin forgiving your parents. You can forgive the people and not their actions. Then you need to forgive yourself. Learning to forgive yourself can prove to be the hardest forgiveness lesson of all. Stop beating yourself up for messing up your relationship(s), and vow, from this day forward, to do better. When you learn from your mistakes, you begin to live in a world where "It's all good."

7) Our own fear of abandonment keeps us stuck in unhappy relationships—Toxic relationships have an unconscious contract that states: no matter what you do or I do, we'll never abandon each other. This means that you can throw acid in my face, and I can torpedo you, but we never leave each other. Have you ever wondered why you or someone you knew took someone back after that person did unspeakable things? Recognizing this unconscious contract and overcoming our own fears of abandonment are the first steps in breaking away from the magnetic hold that toxic love has over us. When we judge others who have stayed in bad relationships—for example, our own parents—it dooms us to be given this same experience over and over again, until we learn to relinquish judgment of others. In the history of the world, a lot of people have taken a lot of crap in the name of love, and that's the way it was, but it doesn't have to be the way it is or the way of the future.

8) Fear of what people will say or do—Whether you like to admit it or not, fearing judgment and caring what others think or say about you is a form of narcissism. If you're staying unhappily married because you fear what your relatives, friends, business associates, church members, or others will say about you, then recognize the narcissism in that kind of disordered thinking. If your intentions in leaving a particular relationship are pure and coming from a place of deep soul-searching and inner guidance, then what people have to say about your choice should be of no concern to you. Oftentimes, *The Great Enablers*, who have never bad-mouthed their partners during their relationships, have trouble dealing with all the questions surrounding a breakup. When people ask you why you're separating, divorcing, or cutting a person out of your life, you can answer them by asking, "Am I a good person?" These people will invariably respond, "Yes, of course." Then you simply state, "Then I must have my reasons."

The discussion almost always ends there. You're not under obligation to answer questions that, for the most part, are nobody's business but your own.

9) Poor self-esteem issues—If we were raised to think that love is pain and love is abuse, and that we deserve this kind of treatment for the sin of having been born into that family, we will develop poor self-esteem. It doesn't matter how successful we become in the outside world, if in the deepest core of our being we feel unlovable and unworthy. *The Unfixables* scope out these kinds of people, lure them in, and then beat them into submission with every manipulation technique under the sun. A person who already has battered self-esteem now takes on additional systematic beatings, which makes it a herculean task for this broken person to gather the strength to move on. If this is the situation that you're currently drowning in, then try doing some things to foster better self-esteem. Take better care of your physical body. Work out, eat properly, and try kicking some of your bad health habits. Seek therapy or a support group. Make some new friends and keep surrounding yourself with love-minded people. *The Unfixables* love to chisel away at our self-esteem and convince us that we're lucky to have them, and that no one would ever put up with us. See this as their way of keeping you stuck, and turn a deaf ear to that kind of nonsense!

10) You've been raised in a certain culture or by a certain religion that led you to believe that divorce is morally wrong—Individuals who religiously and to a T follow all the dogma of their particular faith may truly believe that they have signed on with their spouses until death do they part, come hell or high water, and that's what their God would expect them to do. This thinking is understandable in the context of their particular frame of reference. Again, reread the above two sentences carefully. The key is that you have to follow your religious beliefs unfalteringly in every circumstance in your life, and there can be no hypocrisy in your thoughts, deeds, and actions as far as picking and choosing what pieces of dogma you follow or don't follow. For example, you were raised Catholic, and that's why you tell others that you can't get a divorce. However, if you've ever used contraceptives, or if you've ever had an abortion, or if you don't go to church every Sunday, or if you've broken any of the other dogmatic teachings of the Catholic Church, then that thinking doesn't wash with the universe as being truth. It just makes the complex decision process of whether to stay or leave your marriage a simple black-and-white one for you. Don't just hide behind dogmatic thinking to stay put in a toxic relationship. Do you truly believe that God would want someone to stay in a marriage where one person is enabling another, abusing another, or causing great angst and heartbreak to another? If you've fallen for the Prince or Princess Who Became a Beast, then this would be considered a fraudulent contract. Therefore, you have the right to terminate this marriage in the most karmically correct way possible, which means striving for divorce without drama and trauma. Once again, love yourself the way you love or would love your own child. If you would tell your beloved child to stay married to a similar person, then that's what you can truthfully tell yourself to do. However, if you'd tell your child to run for the hills and never look back, then that's exactly what you can, in good conscience, tell yourself to do as well.

11) Toxic Love is an Addiction—Have you ever judged other people's addictions? Have you ever wondered why they just can't give up drinking, gambling, sexing, overspending, smoking, overeating, or drugging? If you've been guilty of this kind of black-and-white thinking, the universe will call you on your judgments by showing you that even people who think that they're not prone to addictions can and do get hooked on toxic love.

Once a love affair turns toxic, a whole series of dysfunctional behaviors start happening, and the relationship begins spiraling downhill. Then the unconscious contract, which is always a part of toxic love, starts kicking in. This contract states, "No matter what you do or I do, we never abandon each other." After a while, you might start feeling that this relationship isn't good for you, but you get hooked into all the drama and breaking away becomes more and more difficult.

When you finally do break away, you start getting all the same feelings, psychologically, emotionally, and physically, that you would experience if you were trying to detox from drugs. You can't sleep. You can't eat. You can't concentrate. You feel sick to your stomach and your head hurts. You feel depressed, anxious, paranoid about what your ex may be doing, and out of control. You give into these feelings and call your ex. Like a drug addict, you need a fix. After seeing this person, in record time you remember why you're trying to break away. You start kicking yourself in the head for falling off the wagon and going back. You feel guilty and worried. If this person is a cheater or intravenous drug user, sleeping with him or her could put you in harm's way or even be the death of you, should you contract HIV. If he or she is violent and irrational, you know that you are truly putting your life on the line, and you further beat yourself up about your behavior.

If your relationship has become a toxic addiction, then going cold turkey may be the best way to go. No texting, talking, booty calls, or contact has to be the rule.

By the way, love can be fixed by putting two feet completely into a relationship or by taking two feet out. The one-foot-in-and-one-foot-out thing that people do for years fixes nothing. If you're not sure if you should stay in your current relationship or leave it, then try putting two feet completely back in. Love this person as best you can with your entire heart, soul, mind, and body for three months. (If during this time the love turns violent or abusive, all bets are off.) If nothing changes at the end of three months, then you'll have to try taking two feet out. In taking two feet out, this doesn't mean the relationship is over. If the two of you seek separate counseling and work at dealing with your own healing issues, you could conceivably return to each other ready, willing, and able to love and commit to your relationship. The entire universe rejoices when this rare, but miraculous, event occurs!

Have you noticed that all of the above reasons, purposes, and payoffs in staying in bad relationships are fear-based ones? God is asking all of us, in this new millennium, to walk the path of love. In walking away from bad relationships, we're trying to save our own souls and to better the quality of life for ourselves and for everyone else while we're still here on earth.

When all is said and done, the main reason good people can't leave bad relationships is this one simple truth: they haven't healed their own issues. Taking time to deal with your own stuff and owning your own baggage and carrying it are a few of the most important things you can do to prepare yourself for better relationships at work, at play, in families, and in love affairs. Heal thyself.

Spend the next few days examining your own fears and how they're keeping you trapped in victim consciousness. What steps do you need to overcome your fears? Come up with a step-by-step plan that will help you strategically work your way out of any relationship, whether at work or at home, that you know in your heart of hearts isn't serving your or their higher good.

Some of the Oldest Tricks in the Book That Keep People Tied to Bad Relationships

1. **Women get pregnant:** Whether this act is committed consciously or sub-consciously, the outcome is the same—a child is born into dysfunction. If you have a fear of abandonment, then this trick keeps you tied to this toxic relationship for a long time, if not for the rest of your life, because you share this child together. If your relationship is in trouble, think twice before engaging in unprotected sex or having sex without being sure that at least one of you, and better yet, both of you, are using some form of contraception. No child wants to be the crazy glue that was created to hold two broken people together.

2. **You make yourself sick:** There's no denying that there's a very strong mind/body connection. I have seen this pattern all too often: When my clients, who just happen to be some of *The Great Enablers,* finally muster up the nerve to leave a toxic relationship, all of a sudden they come down with an autoimmune disorder or some other mysterious disease. The next thing I know, they're telling me that they can't leave the relationship now because they're too sick to move on. This illness might leave them unable to work, and they feel that they can't leave anytime soon because they can no longer support themselves. Worse yet, just as *The Great Enablers* get the courage to move on, *The Unfixables* get a major illness or feign one, and then *The Great Enablers* feel too guilty to move on. They end up staying to take care of these people who don't do anything to help themselves get better because they know that *The Great Enablers* will never leave them when they're down.

3. **Screwing up the finances so that you can't afford to leave:** Sometimes people, good ones and not-such-good ones, sabotage their efforts or their partners' efforts to break free from toxic relationships by screwing up the finances. They gamble away the money, spend too much, spend long periods unemployed, and somehow this couple always finds themselves in debt. This keeps both people enslaved to the relationship, because neither one of them can afford to leave.

Whether these tricks are consciously or subconsciously performed makes no difference. The outcome is still the same: people stay stuck in bad relationships.

The Good, the Bad, and the Ugly of *The Good-to-a-Fault People*

The Good-to-a-Fault People serve many valid purposes on this earth. At times, they're beacons of light for others to see. Their unselfish, kind, trusting, giving ways make the journey for others on this earth much more bearable. It's only when *The Good-to-a-Fault People* can't see how they're being *The Great Enablers* that the trouble begins. *The Good-to-a-Fault People* cease to be good examples of behavior when they:

- enable others
- continually rescue *The Unfixables*
- carry other people's crosses
- clean up everyone else's mess

In the above instances, they're not the solution to a manipulative, unkind, and unjust world; they're part of the problem.

For as long as you walk this earth, you'll be tested again and again. God will give you life experiences that will force you to choose time and time again: *Do you want to be part of the solution, or do you want to be part of the problem?*

Karmic Lessons *The Good-to-a-Fault People* Still Need to Learn

1. **To stop trying to fix people**—It's an insult to God for you to think that you can fix others. God is up there trying to figure out what wake-up calls to give all of us, never quite sure which ones will or won't work. Our spirit guides, angels, deceased loved ones, and God all try to figure out: *What in the world should we do now? Should we give this person a new job? Should we keep him unemployed? Should we give her a major illness or a minor one? Should we grant her a miracle? Should we throw the bastard in jail? Should we bring her a Soul Mate? Should we nuke her house in a hurricane or should we "pass over" her house?* What will or won't change someone is ultimately up to the free will of that person. If God knows and can accept this, then isn't it narcissistic of us to think otherwise? "Behold, we are going to Jerusalem. The Son of Man will be delivered to the chief priest and the scribes. They will condemn him to death, and will deliver him to the Gentiles" (Mark 10:33). When Jesus made this statement, it was the third time that he revealed the knowledge of his own impending death. Jesus was letting his disciples know that he understood that he could not fix or change *The Unfixables,* and that they would soon put an end to him. Then who was Jesus here to awaken? I believe he came to awaken *The Good-to-a-Fault People;* to let them know that it wasn't their job to carry the crosses of *The Unfixables;* but rather, it was his.

2. **To trust your gut**—If your gut tells you something isn't kosher, then something isn't kosher. Don't wait to have your face smeared in crap before you realize this. If you think someone is lying to you, cheating on you, or betraying you, then they are. You don't need to stick around and wait until you catch venereal disease, or until you see that your bank account has been emptied. Listen to your own inner voice and the voice of divine guidance that's always trying to keep you two steps ahead of everything. You don't have to keep giving everyone the benefit of the doubt!

3. **To stop just seeing the good in everyone**—Learn to see what is truly in front of your face.

4. **To be loyal to people who deserve your loyalty**—One of the hardest lessons you'll ever have to learn is how and when to walk away from people, and how and when to punish those who deserve that treatment.

5. **To come to the deep realization that everything isn't your fault**—Therefore, it isn't your job to clean up everybody's messes and carry everyone else's crosses.

6. **To know what true forgiveness is**—Forgiveness isn't a free pass for others to abuse you. Forgiveness is a long, hard process. Bypassing any of the steps to forgiveness keeps true justice from taking place on this earth.

7. **To know what peace truly means**—Peace isn't shutting the hell up. It isn't walking away from a situation without first doing something to right a wrong.

Remember: Certain relationships have a limited shelf life. If you keep them beyond their expiration dates, don't be surprised when they turn sour, or worse yet, rotten right before your very eyes.

Remember: It's our own judgments that truly keep us trapped. Until we stop judging others, we will be imprisoned by the same stifling mind-set.

Questions for Self-Analysis

1. Have you ever relived your parents' marriage? Did you do this more than once? Did you ever take on the role of your mother? Did you ever take on the role of your father?

2. Have you ever been in a toxic relationship that felt like an addiction? Are you currently in one?

3. What issues do you still need to heal? What can you do to heal them?

4. Which of the reasons, purposes, or payoffs in staying in a bad relationship resonates the most with you?

5. What tricks have you played on yourself to keep you trapped in toxic relationships?

6. What tricks have others played on you to keep you trapped in toxic relationships?

Epilogue

...With God all things are possible.

—Matthew 19:26

For most of my adult life, I felt like I was stuck in the mud and going nowhere fast. At one point, I felt that if I didn't start doing something to change my life, I was going to fall into the life-threatening, bottomless pit of deep depression. In the very core of my being, I knew that I couldn't keep seeing a hopeless future with no chance for happiness, or I would surely die of a broken heart or one day blow my brains out with a stroke. I repeatedly told myself that I would have to envision a better life for myself some way, somehow, even if I had no idea how to make that vision a reality.

Every morning, to motivate myself to get up and face the day, I would play over and over in my mind the comforting scenario of what my ideal life would be like in the future. I did this throughout the day as well, whenever the recurring, tormenting, hopeless thoughts tried to take over my consciousness.

Believe me; I had no idea that I was practicing the Law of Attraction. This law states that we create our world with our thoughts. The Law of Attraction further asks that we visualize what we want. This law does not demand that we immediately know how to acquire those things. I look back with amazement on how my ability to envision a positive future started the ball rolling for me so that the doors of my heart, soul, and mind began opening, and amazing changes began happening.

Throughout those angst-filled years, I had a recurring dream: I dreamed that I lived in a glass house. This glass house had no windows or doors, but I could see the whole larger world from every direction. I would gaze to the left of me, to the right of me, behind me, and in front of me, but there was no way out. I stared in awe at that larger world that beckoned me to come and explore new horizons and to shoot for the stars.

Then, one cold winter night in 2004, I had the same dream again, only this time I saw a beautiful angel. She whispered, "Cindi, look in your right hand." I opened my hand and saw a plain old rock, nothing to speak of, for sure. "You've had that rock all along," the beautiful angel said. "What are you waiting for? You're like David with a rock. Just throw it and Goliath will fall."

I gazed upon that rock again, and right before my very eyes, it instantly changed into a huge diamond. To my amazement, without a moment's hesitation, I threw it. The house shattered, and I was free.

After decades of great inner anguish and indecision, I was able to change my life. When we're clear in our intentions, and when we can see a better future, miracles happen.

Learn to live in yesterday's tomorrow—learn to live for today.

And, of course, let's end this book on a happily-ever-after note. That ideal life that I had imagined, dreamed of, wished for once upon a time has become my reality.

If I can have it, then you—most certainly—can have it, too. Aim for the stars and settle for nothing less than bliss.

See...Believe...Break Free...

Printed in Great Britain
by Amazon

82580482R00130